Wooden Ships & Iron Men

The Story of the Schooner Fronie Myrtle

Maxwell Rowe & Suzanne Wheeler

We gratefully acknowledge the financial support of the Canada Council for the Arts, the Government of Canada through the Canada Book Fund (CBF), and the Government of Newfoundland and Labrador through the Department of Tourism, Culture and Recreation for our publishing program.

Cover Design by Todd Manning
Layout by Joanne Snook-Hann
Back Cover Painting by Jackie Evans, 1997
Printed on acid-free paper

Published by
CREATIVE PUBLISHERS
an imprint of CREATIVE BOOK PUBLISHING
a Transcontinental Inc. associated company
P.O. Box 8660, Stn. A
St. John's, Newfoundland and Labrador A1B 3T7

Printed in Canada

Rowe, Maxwell
Wooden ships & iron men : the story of the schooner Fronie Myrtle / Maxwell Ross Rowe, Suzanne E. Wheeler.

ISBN 978-1-77103-014-4

1. Fronie Myrtle (Schooner). 2. Fishers--Newfoundland and Labrador--Biography. 3. Seafaring life--Newfoundland and Labrador. I. Wheeler, Suzanne II. Title. III. Title: Wooden ships and iron men.

VM395.F76R68 2013 387.2'2 C2013-901002-5

Wooden Ships & Iron Men

The Story of the Schooner Fronie Myrtle

Maxwell Rowe & Suzanne Wheeler

CREATIVE PUBLISHERS

St. John's, Newfoundland and Labrador
2013

To the Skipper and Crew

of the

Fronie Myrtle

(1935 - 1949)

TABLE OF CONTENTS

I was two yr old when my Father builded the Schooner "Francis Myrtle" I can't recall much of the building but I remember I was five yr old when I took my first trip. And I remember that quite clearly. I was attending School at the time and it wasn't strange to have a Feathered "Flea" in your head more especially with my black hair. My Father would say if there was two there I would be sure to pick up one. So after we pulled up anchor at Lahave Cove and headed for "Fauver Seer Hi" my Father would set me down in front of him while he was steering the Schooner and clean my head before he would let me sleep in one of the Bunks

PREFACE

I remember a particular day during the early spring of 2009 when I was driving along the highway to my home in Grand Falls-Windsor, Newfoundland. I was thinking about my father and grandfather and their beloved schooner, the *Fronie Myrtle.* As their stories about the ship and its crew came flooding back to me, I wondered about writing a book that would celebrate the schooner, its crew, and the remarkable men who built it and sailed it in the waters off Newfoundland and Labrador. At the time, however, I only had a few memories based on the stories told by my grandfather, William Rowe (1895 – 1978), and my father, Maxwell Rowe (1933 – 2010). That was enough material to get me started on the project, but I would need much more.

During the late spring and early summer of 2009, I wrote a brief outline of what I thought the narrative might entail. Then I jotted down a few questions, bought myself a hardcover notebook, and I began my writing journey. The first task was to find an opportune time to convince my dad about the plan. With vacations and travel, the summer months passed by quickly and there was no chance even to mention the idea. Then fate intervened. At the beginning of September, dad suddenly became ill. I spent the week of September 13 – 20 with him in the ironically named Chance Cove before we were given the diagnosis. He was stricken with cancer, although in his case the disease was supposed to be highly curable.

At the beginning of that same week, I had asked him about working with me to write the story of the *Fronie Myrtle.* Fortunately, he was very excited about the idea, and we spent the next seven days talking about the schooner.

Actually, I mostly *listened.* Dad had a fantastic memory; he was also a great storyteller. I quickly realized he had a great deal of valuable material that would help me recreate the life and times of the schooner and her crew. (He also had a good idea about where I could find other helpful information, too.) During the fall and winter months while he was receiving the chemotherapy treatments, dad wrote down everything he could remember about the *Fronie Myrtle.* Each time I visited, I would give him another list of questions, although he would never show me his notebook. Finally, during one of my many visits to Chance Cove, my dad passed the notebook to me.

"This is it," he said. He had tears in his eyes and I knew it had been a struggle for him physically to write as much as he did. Many days he hardly had the strength to hold a pen, but he persevered until he had recorded all he could remember about the *Fronie Myrtle.*

I left my parent's house with the precious notebook, took it home, and began to piece everything together. During breaks from that work, I also talked to family members, did research into our family history, checked online resources, and collected photographs and historical documents from relatives of the crewmen. Every time I visited dad, his first question was always "How's the book coming along?" Finally, when I had a draft prepared, I plucked up my courage and went to visit dad – who was now at my sister's house in Corner Brook. Even though he was extremely ill, he was eager to read the manuscript.

When he finished reading the manuscript on April 20, once again he had tears in his eyes. He told me he was *extremely* pleased with my draft of the story.

"People forget what you tell them," he said. "But a book stays around for a long time." Then he handed the stack of pages back to me. A few weeks later, on June 3, 2010, my dad passed away.

With the help of my father and many others, this is our account of the life of the schooner *Fronie Myrtle* and its gallant crew.

NOTE TO READERS

I have tried to explain any unfamiliar words within the actual context of the narrative. However, readers who may be unfamiliar with nautical terms or phrases used in Newfoundland and Labrador may wish to consult the Glossary at the end of the book. Anyone who is *really* keen to learn more about our culture and language may wish to consult the *Dictionary of Newfoundland English, Second Edition with Supplement.* It is available in both print and online versions from the University of Toronto Press.

INTRODUCTION

"Will we get a load of fish this summer?
No one can answer that yet,
but we have faith – and faith can load the schooner itself."

Those were the inspiring words of my uncle, Eli William Rowe. His sentiments echoed the faith of many schooner crewmen and skippers. In the spring, they left their homes behind and embarked on long summer trips along the coastal waters of Labrador. In those frigid seas they hoped to catch enough fish to sell for cash so they could have provisions for the winter. It was a risky proposition on all counts. Seamen on modern ships have sophisticated navigational systems. My grandfather Will and his crew had only crude instruments to guide them. Mostly they relied on reports from other fishing vessels and on the skills passed down from generations of other sailors.

View of lower Chance Cove harbour from the hill behind William Rowe's house, with the sawmill and shop to the left, and Samuel Rowe's house to the far right.

The period in history when schooners fished off the Labrador coast remains an important part of our Newfoundland heritage. My own schooner heritage goes back to 1783 when my ancestor James Rowe purchased property in Heart's Content and built a dock. This was the beginning of more than 100 years of shipbuilding undertaken by Rowe, his sons, and eventually his grandsons. The lineage is worth noting. James Rowe was the son of Edward Rowe who moved to Trinity from England in the mid-1700's. James later moved from Trinity to Hearts Content, where he had five daughters and six sons. One of his sons, born in 1785, was also named James and he opened a second shipbuilding dock in Witless Bay (now called Whiteway). James was the father of Benjamin Rowe (1833-1907), and one of his sons was Eli Rowe (1870-1908), who died quite young. His son, in turn, was my grandfather, William Rowe. William had a son, also named Eli, and his diary is included in this book. My father, Max, was proud of this long heritage of fine ship-builders.

The *Fronie Myrtle* was built in Chance Cove in 1935, and she sailed out of that port until 1949. Not only is this the story of the *Fronie Myrtle*, but it is also the account of the men whose lives were intertwined with the schooner's birth, adventurous life, and sad ending. To the best of my knowledge, there are still two crew members alive. William Smith, also from Chance Cove, is living in Ontario, according to his brother Nathan Smith of Chance Cove. Winston Rowe, Samuel Rowe's son, was born in 1935. He accompanied his father on short trips to St. John's in the late 1940's. Winston currently lives in British Columbia.

Although the schooner and the rest of the crew are gone, they speak to us through the remembered stories of hard work, misadventures, and sometimes prosperous journeys. Like a time capsule, there are treasures in this book that bring us back to the old schooner fishing days in outport Newfoundland. These stories are all part of the history that makes us who we are today.

Beginnings

If we are to believe the nautical stories passed down through the generations, the first vessel to be called a schooner was created by shipbuilder Andrew Robinson and launched in Gloucester, Massachusetts, in 1713. Legend has it that the name was the result of a spectator exclaiming, "Oh, how she scoons." ("Scoon" was a Scottish term that meant "to skip or skim over the water.") Robinson boldly replied, "A schooner let her be."

A schooner has two or more masts rigged fore-and-aft, and its sail design allows for high speed and extreme maneuverability. Sailors like to say that a schooner can lie "closer to the wind" than square-rigged sailing ships. The vessel also needs a smaller crew to handle the rigging, even though some schooners may have up to seven masts. Schooners were first constructed in colonial America and because of their speed became one of the favourite craft in the United States and Canada during the latter half of the 18th century and the first half of the 19th century. The classic Canadian schooner was the famous *Bluenose,* which was built in 1921 and replicated in 1963 as the *Bluenose II.* That ship has recently been refitted and readied for further adventures.

There have been many variations of schooner design and sail rigging to suit an equal number of purposes. In Newfoundland, two-masted schooners were the most preferred sailing vessel for fishing and cargo. Schooners were the lifeline of the early settlements, connecting distant outports with the larger supply centres of the province. Schooners were widely used in the North Atlantic fisheries and the North American coastal trade until World War I, when they were often replaced by power-driven craft. In Newfoundland and Labrador, however, the schooner tradition carried on for many decades. Some maritime scholars say that schooners were the sturdiest and most adaptable ship of all time. This was the proud heritage my family continued when they set out to build the *Fronie Myrtle* almost eighty years ago.

The years when the *Fronie Myrtle* were on the water corresponded almost exactly to the period when the Newfoundland Commission of Government (1934-1949) was in power. During this fifteen-year term, they offered various incentives to help build the economy and get people back to work during the Great Depression. One of those incentives was meant to assist boat-builders and fishermen. In response to the Commission's thirty-dollar-per-ton shipbuilding bounty in the mid-1930's, there was a revival of Newfoundland schooner construction. With abundant wood supply, and plenty of available labour, the incentive began to do its work. In areas of the coast where the Labrador fishery was still viable, a number of small schooners were soon being built. Many of them would remain in use until the end of World War II.

In 1934, my grandfather Will Rowe applied to the Commission of Government for a loan to build one of these fishing schooners. The first instalment of $350.00 was enough to start the project, and another $350.00 was acquired partway through the construction. At the time, the risks involved in this venture were enormous. The economy was desperate and people were suffering. Chance Cove was a poor community with a population of 288 people (according to the 1935 Census), who depended mostly on fishing and logging for their livelihood. Neither occupation was very profitable.

Before he built the *Fronie Myrtle,* Will made a modest living by whatever work he could sustain. He fished inshore with a small motor-boat. He worked as a sawmill operator. And together with his wife, Phoebe, he operated a general store. (The general store actually stayed active until the late 1960's.) Will decided to build the schooner because he knew there was the possibility of more fish off the coast of Labrador. He simply needed a larger vessel. He also knew he could use the schooner for delivering freight, especially to those places that were inaccessible by road. This had proven workable for his uncle Samuel Rowe who had a schooner called the *Melva Abbie* from 1906 to 1914, when she was lost at Northern Bay. Everyone seemed to be connected by schooners. My grandfather Will had an uncle Samuel referenced here, and he had a brother Sam who was part owner of the *Fronie Myrtle.* There were other ancestors in Hearts Content who had a dock where they built schooners. In fact, there is apparently still a "Rowe Dock" in that town.

With these examples before him, Will set about the task of building a schooner. Four types of wood were needed for the *Fronie Myrtle.* Birch was used below the water line. It is a hard and dense wood that is less susceptible to rot and sea-worms. B.C. fir, which was purchased in St. John's and brought to Chance Cove by boat, was used for the masts and booms. Spruce was used for timbers in most of the ship, while locally cut fir was used for all the planks above the water-line and for the decking.

Except for the B.C. fir, every piece of wood was cut in the Trinity Bay area during the four-month period it took to build the schooner. In fact, the logs were pulled out of the woods by horse and sleigh and then brought to Chance Cove in boats. Will had a Bulldog sawmill engine, which he used to cut the lumber at his mill in Chance Cove. The woodcutters, all from Chance Cove, were Adam Smith, Chesley Smith, Benjamin Rowe, Alfred Rowe, Levi Rowe, Noah Rowe, Kenneth Brace, and Charles Rowe. They felled the trees around Rantem, down the Arm, and on the East side of the Arm.

Sometimes the men needed particular shapes of wood for various parts of the schooner. They would then set to work making moulds from thin pieces of wood to match the shape of the piece they needed. Usually, these were for some of the curved parts, such as in the stern or bow where they wanted a single piece of wood already in the correct shape. They took these wooden moulds into the woods, and when they found a tree that looked promising they compared the shape. Sometimes they had to dig the tree out with a pick and shovel in order to get a piece in the shape of an elbow, for example, which would be infinitely stronger than anything fashioned in that shape from two separate pieces of wood.

My grandfather Will cut one piece of timber used in the stern with a Red Rover axe – and people still talk about how he did it. For this part of the ship, Will needed to have a particular shape of wood. During the time when they were cutting the timber, he spotted a tree in the shape he was looking for – but it was partway down a cliff on a ledge and about fifty feet from the water. It was growing out and up, just the right shape. So two men from the top of the cliff lowered him down to the tree on a rope, and he cut the tree with the axe. When it fell in the water, the men retrieved it by boat. As Will had predicted, it was the perfect shape for the stern of the schooner.

Almost every place in Newfoundland had their own boat-builder, especially for vessels from 15 feet to 30 feet long. My dad Max remembered one winter when the men built as many as six motor-boats and skiffs from 24 feet to 30 feet long. He knows this as fact because he sawed every piece of timber and plank that went into boats from the sawmill he owned and operated. It was a very busy time and he worked long hours in the mill each day. The woodcutters started cutting the trees in the fall of 1934. The Commission of Government Indenture documents were signed in December, 1934, and the schooner was ready to sail in the spring of 1935. Considering the size of the ship, where the materials had to come from, and the type of tools used, it was amazing how the men managed to complete the schooner in such a short time.

There were a number of carpenters besides my grandfather, Will, who worked on the *Fronie Myrtle*, and they were almost all from Chance Cove. There was Sam Rowe, Will's younger brother, who lived across the road from him in Chance Cove. There was also Bramwell Brace (better known as Bram), as well as Gordon Brace, who later both became crewmen. Benjamin Rowe, Alfred Rowe, William Smith, and Nelson Allen were all carpenters from Chance Cove. However, because of the boat's size, Will brought in an experienced schooner builder, Lorenzo Simmons, from Green's Harbour.

The carpenters were paid $2.50 a day and they put in long hours of hard work to earn those wages. Bram Brace verified to his great-grandson Mark that he remembers walking with Alfred Rowe five miles each way to the train at Rantem Station to bring nails to the workers. He carried the fifty-pound bag on his back – and then he returned for another one. Each round-trip took him almost five hours. This strong and hardy group knew what hard work was all about!

During the building of the schooner, my dad's sister Melva was in her teens and she was as pretty as a picture. Naturally, the men working at the boat would joke and carry on with her. Melva was not shy. In fact, there was a fair bit of lively banter. One day while she was picking up wood chips for the fire, she spotted Little Jake behind a pile of wood "making his water."

Melva teased, "I see you."

Little Jake answered, "I don't care, you never seen a *batter* (better)."

Many of the men at this time smoked the pipe or chewed tobacco, and some did both at the same time. It was a common habit in those days. The most popular brand was Beaver tobacco, which was made locally in St. John's at the Imperial Tobacco Plant on the corner of Bond and Flavin Streets. Chewing tobacco came in a rectangular block about six inches by two inches and about one inch thick. They called it a plug of tobacco, and it cost around twenty-five cents. My uncle Ed remembers that the plug of tobacco had the name "Beaver" spelled across it. Sometimes, the shop-keeper cut between each letter and sold it in sections to the men. This was called "selling it by the letter."

One colourful fellow named "Black Bill" was famous for chewing tobacco wherever he worked. You could see chews of tobacco stuck in the corners of the wood where he left them for another day. "Black Bill" was remembered for other habits and mishaps as well. My grandfather told dad one story with a tear *and* a twinkle in his eye. In order to get the schooner ready for the upcoming fishing season, my grandfather had hired some of the local small-boat builders

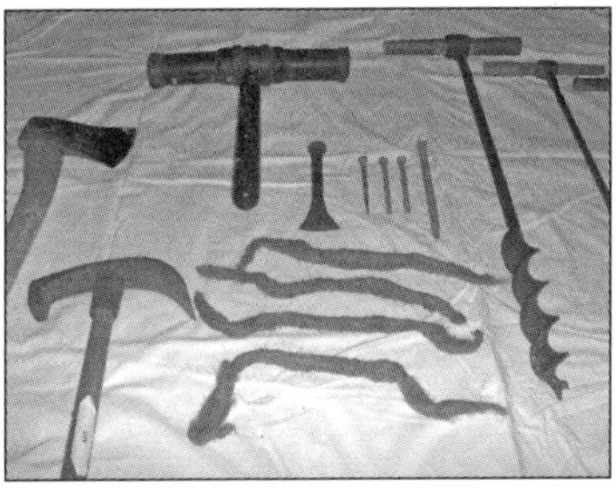

Spokeshave, Hammer, Augers, Gimlet, Planes, Axe, Adze, Mallets, Square Nails, Caulking Iron, Oakum.

The carpenters used all of the tools pictured – plus some handsaws – in the building of the schooner. My uncle Ed has kept them for the family. Photos by S. Wheeler

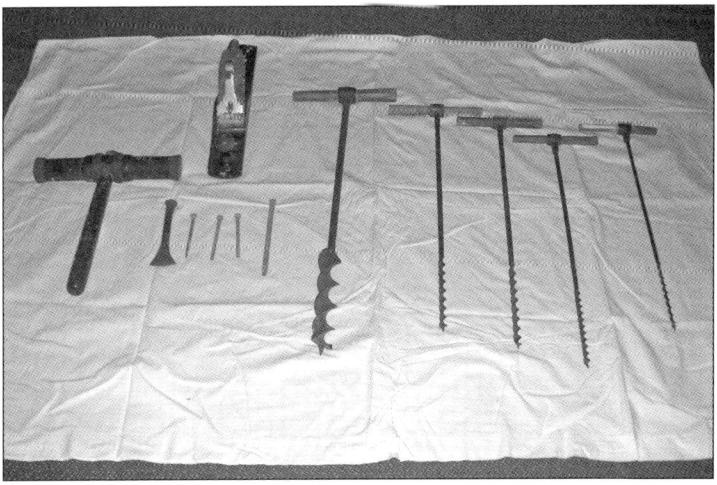

to help those who were more highly skilled. One of those fellows was this same "Black Bill."

When they had the entire outside plank installed up to the bulwarks, the local builder (Black Bill) told my grandfather he did not like a certain piece of plank that the professional builder installed. He said it was a rough job; it did not look right. For a full week, every time my grandfather crossed "Black Bill" near this piece of plank, he would make some comment about it. Near the end of the week, Mr. Simmons, the schooner builder, went home for a few days. He had no sooner left when "Black Bill" came to my grandfather again complaining about this piece of plank. My grandfather said, "For God's sake Bill, if you don't like it, go and change it." My grandfather told dad that "Black Bill" took out the piece of plank and installed a new piece. When he had it finished, the plank fit so well you hardly had to caulk it. For many years afterwards, when my grandfather pulled the skiff up to the side of the schooner, that piece of plank stood out in his mind.

This kind of expert work was doubly hard because there were not many tools available. There were certainly no electric tools; everything was cut and sawed by hand. The carpenters' tools included augers (used for drilling holes), gimlets (small augers), planes, handsaws, axe, adze (curved axe), hammers, mallets, square-headed galvanized nails, oakum (a fibrous material used to caulk the openings between the planks), caulking iron (used to push the oakum between the planks), and a spokeshave (a type of plane for shaping and smoothing the wood).

Dad could not recall the building work on the *Fronie Myrtle,* of course, because he was born in 1933, just a year before the planning. For the *Fronie Myrtle's* first season in 1935, he was only two years old. However, when he was six years old, his father allowed him to go on short trips for freight delivery. My dad Max was fourteen when he had his first fishing trip on the schooner. This was in 1947. Curiously, he remembered something of greater fascination to a young child. Dad had lice in his lovely black hair. His father would say, "If there were two [lice] around, Max would be sure to pick one up." So, after they pulled anchor at Chance Cove and headed for Lower Deer Harbour, my grandfather would set dad down in front of him while steering the schooner. He insisted on cleaning my father's head before he would let him sleep in one of the bunks. He was proud of the boat, and he wasn't prepared to have lice on board the ship – not after all the time, money, and hard work he had invested.

Although my grandfather Will was a boat-builder and his ancestors before him, his own father Eli died when my grandfather was nine years old. So the skills to build the *Fronie Myrtle* must have come down through his father's genes. Although my grandfather never went to school, he was highly intelligent and self-taught. My grandmother Phoebe, who was a schoolteacher, contributed to my grandfather's learning, especially in reading, writing, and mathematics (called arithmetic then), which enabled him to conduct business matters related to fishing, shipping, and building the *Fronie Myrtle*. One of those skills was the outfitting of the vessel. Cutting the sails and sewing them together, for example, required a special talent. The size and shape had to be exact or the schooner would not sail right. Sailors would say a ship was "hard to answer to" when tacking or entering a harbour.

Will Rowe bought the first set of canvas sails in St. John's. It turned out that this set was too small, however, and it had to be replaced after the first summer's fishing. My grandfather did not make the same mistake twice. The next set of sails fit the *Fronie Myrtle* perfectly. They made her one of the fastest schooners on the water. The man who fashioned those sails was Joseph (Joe) Reid from Little Harbour East, Placentia Bay. There were hundreds of schooners in Placentia Bay in the 1930's. This gave Mr. Reid many opportunities to learn his trade well. My grandfather was extremely satisfied with this second set of sails and the way the boat handled with them. Meanwhile, Mr. Reid gave up the sail-making business when roads were constructed across the province. He became a foreman with the highway crews, while out on the water the world of schooners was slowly coming to an end.

In 1934, they had completed the woodcutting and received the approvals from the Commission of Government. In the spring of 1935, they completed the construction of the *Fronie Myrtle* and rigged her for sailing. The schooner was fitted with these five sails: a mainsail, foresail, jumbo, outside jib, and a topsail. The *Fronie Myrtle* was built to plans recommended by the Commission of Government according to the size and tonnage required for fishing and hauling supplies. Will customized the finishing details, however, and he painted the schooner a dark green with brown canvas sails. On completion, the vessel was a 69-foot long, 39-ton schooner. She could easily carry an average of 600 quintals of fish, although there were seasons when she carried more than 800 quintals, and according to Bram Brace possibly as much as 1000 quintals. (A quintal is a measurement of fish roughly equivalent to

51 kilograms or 112 pounds.) To do all this work, the *Fronie Myrtle* was fitted for a crew of seven men and provisions.

They named her *Fronie Myrtle* after Will Rowe's youngest daughter, Fronie, and Samuel Rowe's oldest daughter, Myrtle. Will had three other daughters – Stella, Melva, and Carrie – but for reasons unknown to me, he chose his youngest daughter's name for the memorable schooner. Myrtle was the only daughter that Samuel had at the time. The schooner was given the short nickname of *Fronie* by Little Jake (Jacob Smith, Sr.) and, being an unusual name, it stuck. All the crew referred to her this way thereafter. *Fronie* is, indeed, the proper name and spelling. Although it isn't found much on the mainland, it's not an uncommon name in Newfoundland and Labrador.

I can only imagine the day they launched the schooner, with all the community coming together to help her in the water. There would have been men heaving and pulling her with ropes and rolling her along on logs until the *Fronie's* bow and stern were submerged in her new watery home. The proudest of all of them would have been Will Rowe, who may have wondered how she would look in the water and more importantly how she would sail. What a day that must have been!

This was the beginning of a new adventure – and a risky one, too. There was still a mortgage owing to the Commission of Government, plus there were provisions to buy and men to pay. Would they find enough fish? Would they have safe sailing? In the early to mid-1900's, hundreds of schooners met a tragic end on the rocks along the Newfoundland and Labrador coast. The future was uncertain, but these were determined and resilient men and women.

Fronie entering Chance Cove harbour. Submitted by Nancy Rowe Burry

When my grandfather decided to build the schooner several years earlier, he had partnered with his brother Sam as well as two loggers from Chance Cove – Gordon and Bram Brace. However, after the expenses and mortgage were paid, the first few years of the *Fronie* were not profitable. Gordon and Bram decided they could make a better living cutting pulpwood, so they ended the partnership. My grandfather and his brother Sam, however, were determined to make the *Fronie* a profitable venture.

In truth, the ship was more of an *adventure* than a business venture. The courageous stories of the men who sailed the schooner are told in the pages that follow. None were ever lost at sea. And all of them returned safely to shore with stories to tell. In the famous words of Will Rowe, "Well done yourself!"

Sailors & Their Tales

"There's a saying about wooden ships and iron men. Well, there were a few iron boys around also." (Max Rowe)

Each crewman chosen for a voyage had his special area of expertise, which was essential if the expedition was going to be a success. Sailing a schooner from Chance Cove to the Labrador shores without radar or depth-sounder through ice-jams, fog, and extreme weather conditions was not the job for men who couldn't make the right decisions. To make matters even more complicated, the owners could not afford to fit the schooner with a motor for the first two years. Eventually, Will purchased a second-hand gas motor, which they repaired and installed in the schooner. After several more years, he added a second used motor, which he repaired and installed as a back-up.

When my dad was fourteen years old, he was on a trip from Harbour Grace to Chance Cove. The schooner left around dinnertime and had a beautiful trip out of Conception Bay, with a whole sail breeze blowing out of Trinity Bay. When they came through Bacileu Tickle, just after dark, my grandfather figured they would have a good time crossing the bay and headed home. Approximately one hour before 12 o'clock, dad awoke in his bunk with a funny feeling in his stomach. He was never seasick in his life, and heard his father bragging about it. Dad hopped out of the bunk to head for the deck and get some fresh air.

Phoebe and William Rowe. Photo Submitted by Ed Rowe

A young Ed Rowe (called "Eddy" by his Mother).
Photo Submitted by Ed Rowe

Left, Joe Hollet, right, William Rowe, Sr., Skipper of the *Fronie Myrtle*. Photo Submitted by Ed Rowe

A view of the front of William Rowe's house. Photo Submitted by Ed Rowe

Left, William Rowe, Sr., skipper of the *Fronie Myrtle.* Right, Bill Frank Smith, skipper of the *Bernice.* Both were from Chance Cove and are pictured here on a schooner deck at St. John's harbour. (From front cover) Photo Submitted by Ed Rowe

Reg and Eric (dad's twin brothers), who were two years older than dad (which would make them about eighteen) were somewhere above deck. When my dad Max came up from the forecastle, he wandered back toward aft to see who was at the wheel. He told me he remembers it was dark with a fair breeze from the southwest. When dad arrived, he saw his brother Reg at the wheel.

"Who's up forward on watch?" dad asked.

"Eric," Reg replied.

"Where's the rest of the men?"

"Down in their bunks asleep," Reg replied deadpan. There is a saying about wooden ships and iron men that is straight out of the poem "Clipper Ships & Captains" by Rosemary and Stephen Vincent Benet. That poem sums up the character of the men and boys who sailed on the *Fronie* – and on many of the other schooners of the day. They were men of iron will and stamina.

There was a time before our time,
It will not come again,
When the best ships still
were wooden ships,
But the men were iron men.

During the conversations I had with my father, my discussions with Uncle Ed, and through a careful reading of my uncle Bill's diary, we tried to create a complete list of crewmen on the *Fronie Myrtle.* (Some of these men may have crewed for only a single year.) They were an eclectic group of men, often with very little formal education. Still, what they lacked in education they more than made up for in intelligence. They possessed a hefty measure of both common sense and practicality. My grandfather, Will, often conferred with his older hands who had similar experience and with his younger brother Sam, the second-in-command. However, when Will made up his mind, you had better get on board or be left behind. There was no room for argument.

Here is a list of those men:

Bramwell Brace – Cook
Gordon Brace – Crewman
Jim Clarke – Crewman
Walter Peach – Crewman (from Red Harbour)
Jim Peddle – Salter
Stan Peddle – Cook
Ambrose Rowe - Crewman
Eli William Rowe – Crewman (son)
Eric Rowe – Crewman (son)
Maxwell Rowe – Crewman (son)
Reginald Rowe – Crewman, Splitter (son)
Samuel Rowe – Second-in-Command
William Rowe – Skipper
Winston Rowe – Crewman (nephew)
Joseph Smith – Crewman
Thomas K. Smith – Crewman
William Smith – Cook
Eleazor Smith – Crewman
Ernest Smith – Crewman (nephew)
Jacob F. Smith (Little Jake) – Cook
Josiah Smith – Crewman
Eliol Walsh – Crewman (from Sunnyside)
Albert Warren – Crewman (brother-in-law)

In the pages that follow, I have written a short biography of some of the men who my family remembers having served on the *Fronie Myrtle.*

My Grandfather, William Rowe, and his brother Samuel on the bank overlooking Chance Cove harbour. Photo Submitted by Ed Rowe

WILLIAM ROWE 1896-1978

My grandfather William Rowe (1896-1978) was the Skipper of the *Fronie Myrtle*. Except for a brief period early in his marriage to Phoebe when they lived in Red Harbour, he lived in Chance Cove all his life. According to the family tree, the Rowe's originally came from England to Trinity, then to Hearts Content and Chance Cove. Will was born on December 25, 1896. He married Phoebe Peach, formerly from Red Harbour, and they had nine children. He was well respected in the community and was known to be honest in everyday life and business. His skill as a sailor, as a businessman, as a fisherman, and as a hunter helped him to provide a good livelihood for his family even during the difficult days of the Depression. He died on December 24, 1978.

SAMUEL ROWE (SECOND-IN-COMMAND) 1906-1980

Born February 2, 1906, Sam was the younger brother of Will. He lived across the road and was a partner on the *Fronie Myrtle*. When Will was not around, Sam's role changed from Second-in-Command to Skipper, and everyone followed his orders. After his days of the *Fronie,* he bought a car for taxiing. Then he worked in Sept-Iles at the inshore fishery before finishing his career as a Park Ranger. Serving his community in a civic capacity, he held several positions of leadership, one of which was justice of the peace. He died on December 9, 1980.

Samuel Rowe, younger brother to William Rowe the Skipper, and Second-in-Command when my grandfather was not around.
Photo Submitted by Ed Rowe

My father Maxwell Ross Rowe (Crewman) lived a full and adventurous life. Born in Chance Cove, Trinity Bay, on March 16, 1933, he followed in his father's footsteps by sharing in the small general store that the family operated. To supplement his income, he operated a saw-mill and a trucking business. Before starting in the business, Max fished with his father on their schooner out of St. John's. He also had a short stint in the lumber woods working in Terra Nova.

Wanting to better himself, Max started line-work when Checo Engineering began construction of the main transmission lines across Newfoundland. He was successful in obtaining the position of foreman with the company. In

1966, Max was selected to go to Montreal for training on the maintenance of hotlines. Afterwards, he drove back to Newfoundland with his wife, Dot, in the first hotline truck that came into the province. Soon thereafter, he was sent with his good friend Guy Roy to different parts of the island to do specialized work, particularly in substations. For several years while working with Checo, he took the summer months off to captain a tuna boat owned by his brother Reg and which sailed out of Long Pond. Max was very successful and in one year he landed thirty-two tuna.

In the early seventies he started work with the Power Commission as Area Representative. A few years later he accepted a position with Newfoundland Light and Power as Linesman Foreman. Subsequently, he rose to the position of Area Superintendent, working out of Whitbourne. He retired from Newfoundland Power in 1993, but Max continued to live life to the fullest. Although Max and Dot enjoyed travelling and spending time at their Thorburn Lake cabin, Max's greatest joy came from fishing in Chance Cove, hunting, and cutting wood for the winter.

Dad at work.

The fellow who stood out in dad's mind was Jacob F. Smith, known on-board as Little Jake the cook. He was a very short man with a mean temper, but he had the ability to make the *Fronie* sail faster than any of the other crew. Some said he might even have been a better sailor than my grandfather. The harder it blew, the better he liked it. He would take the wheel for his turn even though he was the cook, and he would argue with my grandfather about reefing the sails until the last minute. Here is one of the stories dad remembered.

The *Fronie* had left St. Anthony on the return trip home with decks awash. Some schooners had left an hour ahead of them. When they had gotten so far out, they could see a number of schooners ahead of them. The wind was western with a whole sail breeze. Little Jake strolled up from the forecastle and saw the situation. He said to my grandfather, "Will, I got the kettle boiled. Why don't I give you a spell and you go down and get a cup of tea?"

Although Will was wise to him, he went down for his tea and a little nap. Soon after Will disappeared down the ladder to the forecastle, Little Jake called the two men that were on deck and said, "Boys, get the topmast sail on her." Well, it wasn't very long before the schooners appeared nearer and Little Jake was right in his glee. One of those schooners was always bragging how she could out-sail anything her size. Little Jake was bent on catching her and passing her. This was no easy task, but under the experienced hand of Little Jake, and just a couple of hours before dark, they pulled ahead.

With a chew of tobacco in, he looked behind and said, "You can kiss *Fronie's* behind now." Some thirty years later, he told dad this story with a tear rolling down his cheeks.

My grandfather and my great-uncle Sam were present and nodded in agreement with every word he said.

Josiah (better known as Joe) Smith was another fellow who sailed to Labrador with Will. He was a very quiet man who smoked a pipe, chewed tobacco, and was very humorous. Many times my dad Max laughed until he cried while listening to his stories. On one trip to Labrador they were fishing in Indian Harbour when Joe left his rubber pants on deck. The next morning, when he went to put them on, he discovered they had blown overboard during the night. The next morning, after they hauled the cod traps and salted the fish in the hole, the situation did not look bright for Joe. By this point he was soaking wet. In the following weeks, Joe would now have to do without his rubber pants.

Fishing from a schooner in the Atlantic Ocean is a cold, wet occupation. Rubber pants, or oilskins as they were called, are one of the most important things to have on board. They kept you dry and warm while you hauled nets and processed fish. Sometimes the fishermen bought oilskins pre-made, and sometimes they made them by soaking various pieces of clothing in linseed oil. Normally, they wore oilskin pants that had straps around the shoulders as well as a jacket and hat.

Men could do without a lot of stuff, but rubber pants were not one of them. All the same, these types of people never said die, they never gave up. So, what did Joe do but get one of the cod jiggers and said to Will, "I'm going to try for my pants."

Where they moored was very rough water even without the wind, and sometimes they would have to move until the swell settled down. At the same time, the schooner would swing in an arc approximately 100 feet wide. Now, rubber pants do not sink to the bottom like a rock; they sort of float and sink slowly. So, Joe was hopeful. He threw the jigger over the side of the *Fronie* and hauled back to discover he had hooked a large codfish head. He took the head off and threw the jigger again. When he pulled back on the line, he turned to the crew and said, "Boys, I got them now." The men laughed, but when Joe pulled the jigger over the side, he had his rubber pants hooked to the jigger. Much to his delight and comfort, he did not have to fish without his rubber pants after all.

Albert Warren was married to my grandfather's sister and was from Chapel Arm. He also spent time in Labrador with my grandfather. He was a robust man with great strength. When he would tell something, no matter if it was funny or sad; he would laugh at the end of it. Dad told me he was certain his laugh could be heard two miles away.

Many years after the schooner era, Max met his uncle Albert on the road in Chapel Arm. When he inquired how his aunt Marion was, he said, "Your aunt is not all that well. She fell down the stairs and busted her ankle." At this, he laughed loudly, "HA HA HA!"

Will used to tell a story about Albert that while fishing one summer, the fish were more than plentiful. Every man was full-out from before daylight until after dark. He said that Albert never took off his rubber pants from Monday morning until Saturday night. Now that was a lot of fishing!

Another man whom dad remembered was his cousin Ernest Smith. He fished on the Labrador coast in his late teens, and his job was heading the fish. When the boat arrived at the schooner, one man pronged the fish up on deck, and then up to the splitting table. You had three men working. One cut the throat and ripped his knife down through the middle. This had to be accurate to make it easier for the splitter to remove the bone. The cutter slid the fish to the header, who removed the gut and liver and cracked off the head on a sharp edge made on the table. Then the header slid the fish to the splitter in such a position that the splitter would not have to lose time rearranging the fish. The splitter removed the bone before the fish fell off the table into a tub for washing.

This seems like a drawn-out affair. However, when you had three men who knew what they were doing, it only took a bare second from the time the fish hit the table to when it was in the tub for washing. My grandfather Will was a very fast splitter, and he hated to be kept waiting. In fact, dad often heard him say that Ernest was the only header who could keep him supplied with fish.

After washing, the crew pronged the fish in the hole to the salter. This was a very important job, because each fish had to have the right amount of salt. Jim Peddle was the engineer and the salter. Dad told me he used to be amazed watching him throw the fish five to ten feet and then follow up with a scoop of salt. Fish and salt would land just where he wanted them.

In the thirties, there were hundreds of schooners in Trinity Bay alone, plus schooners from other bays around the island. There would be six to twelve men on each boat. When they all got together in St. John's in the spring and fall, you had a strange mixture of human beings. One who stood out in my dad's memory was William Smith from down the Bay, better known as Large Bill. He weighed more than two hundred pounds and stood over six feet tall. His schooner was another one that more or less travelled with the *Fronie Myrtle.* Bill was a strong and powerful man.

Will told the story how he and Large Bill went for a walk on Water Street one Sunday morning. As they were going up the street, Large Bill's boot came untied. He bent over with his big bum sticking out. At this moment, there was no trouble to see horses and buggies coming and going on Water Street. My grandfather said he saw a shiny buggy coming towards them with the driver sitting up on the seat in front with one of those high black hats on his head and his nose in the air and a whip in his hand.

As he approached them, the driver could see Large Bill's butt staring at him. I guess he could not control the urge, so he whipped Large Bill right on the butt, at the same time lashing the horse so it would move quickly. What he didn't know was that Large Bill was not only big; he was as strong as a bull and fast as a cat. In one split-second after the whip struck him on the butt, Large Bill's hand flew out and grabbed a spoke on the back wheel – just at the same time the whip struck the horse.

Well, sir, the horse made a lunge and Large Bill held the wagon wheel until every spoke fell on the street and the back end of the wagon came down upon the street. The only words that were spoken at that moment came from Large Bill.

"Come on, Will," he said. "Let's finish our walk."

There were other stories about this character. Large Bill, like most sailors, enjoyed a drink of rum. Although there was no money to visit clubs, there was the odd bottle passed around among the schooners. On one such night, Large Bill had consumed a little too much and was four sheets to the wind. While crossing one schooner to get to his own (*The Exotic*), he fell in the water between the two boats and could not get out. After some time passed, a few crewmen who came along heard him thrashing about in the water. However, Large Bill was so heavy, they could not get him out. They made a cry for help and finally some more men arrived. They borrowed a Burton block-and-tackle from one of the schooners, got a rope strapped around him, and eventually they hauled him from the water. When they got Large Bill to the rail of the schooner, three or four men grabbed him and soused him right on the deck.

"Take your time boys," he said, "'cause this is how people gets drowned."

There was one other interesting story Will told my dad about Large Bill. When the schooners arrived from Labrador, the crew off-loaded whatever fish they felt they could handle for washing and drying at the owner's premises. Other smaller communities helped with the drying of the remaining fish. (Fish was off-loaded at different communities for drying because Chance Cove did not have enough flakes to dry the whole catch.) Families at Little Hearts Ease, Deer Harbour, and St. Jones Without sometimes washed and dried the *Fronie*'s fish for 25 cents per quintal.

This would work very well most of the time, but occasionally, through neglect and bad weather conditions, the fish turned out poor. They called this quality of fish "West Indy" because that would be the destination for this kind of catch. The price was very low, not even one quarter of what you could get for good dried fish. The West Indies was also an important market for salt fish from Newfoundland because there were lower tariffs. The merchants relied on the West Indies to sell their poorest grade of salt fish, where it was valued as a cheap source of protein. Coincidentally, the merchants who bought the salt fish in St. John's and sailed to the West Indies brought back rum as well as other goods such as molasses.

On one occasion when the dried salt fish was being off-loaded and culled in St. John's, Large Bill's fish was not doing very well. He questioned the culler about it and gave him a rough time. Three or four schooners were off-loading at the same time as the *Fronie Myrtle*. However, they were doing much better, and this was getting under Large Bill's skin.

He picked up a hard dried fish, about three feet long, which probably weighed about twenty-five pounds and had been culled as a fish for West Indy. He held it up by the fins before the culler's face and said, "Listen, buddy, this fish is not West Indy." Then he ripped the fish right in two from nape to tail. The culler took off like a scalded cat, and they didn't see him again until all the fish were off-loaded.

When the *Fronie Myrtle* returned from a trip to Labrador, the men of Chance Cove would get their muskets out and fire off powder guns to welcome the schooner and crew back home. On one occasion, they arrived in port mid-day, and ninety-nine percent of the people from Chance Cover were watching her come in and moor up. Just down the road from Will's house lived Jim Peddle. He used to sail with my grandfather, but that summer he stayed home. Of course, my dad Max was excited to see the *Fronie* arriving and especially his father, Will. Dad headed down the road towards the part of the cove where the schooner was moored. When dad got near Jim Peddle's house, Jim came running out with his musket. When he saw Max he said, "Come on, I will hold the gun and you pull the trigger." Dad was about seven-years-old at the time.

The men loaded those muskets with only powder and wadding, and when they pulled the trigger there was an awful report. Smoke from the powder covered everything for about fifty feet around. When the gun went off, more than likely the person holding it also went head-over-heels. Dad was very scared, but he was also excited about the return of the *Fronie*. So dad took the chance.

"I will pull the trigger," Max said to Jim, "but you have to hold the gun tight."

"No problem," Jim Peddle said with a sly grin on his face.

Well, sir, dad got right close to him, and when Jim was ready he pulled the trigger. Suddenly Jim went flying through the air with Max on top of him. Dad said he was deaf as a bat from the noise and could not see anything for smoke. When the haze cleared, Jim checked him out to see if he was okay. Then he looked dad in the face and said, "I tell you my son, they heard that one!"

Reg Rowe's widow, Doris (Dodie) Wilcox, told me about a few incidents that involved Reg and his father during voyages to Labrador on the *Fronie Myrtle*. All the sons of William Rowe felt they had to be men in those days. On one of his first trips to these fishing grounds, Reg had a near-fatal accident. As the skiff was put off to haul a net full of fish, Reg was given permission to go along. In the process of hauling the net, however, Reg fell overboard. He told his wife what it felt like. He sank twice and on his third time down, he felt a floating sensation. Then his father grabbed hold of his hand and pulled him in. Reg told this story many times, about how his father saved his life. He also said that all his father could think about after getting Reg back on board was how to explain this to Phoebe, Reg's mother. The loss of a little boy doing a man's job would not be easy to explain.

The trips to Labrador started in the spring and ended in the fall. Reg often spoke about how he and other young lads missed the beginning of the school year. It had an influence on their grades, but not on their desire to learn and succeed in life. Reg learned how to split fish with such great speed and skill that people would gather just to watch him. He was small of stature, but young with fast hands.

His father was much admired, too. Trying to find a safe harbour with an impending storm, for example, was a skill that gained these sailors a certain stature among seamen. While entering a harbour one day, the *Fronie* was caught in very thick fog. Reg's father was so good at sounding the depth and distance that he could make the passage safely while others failed. When the fog lifted, they were safe – but other schooners had wrecked along the shore.

On another occasion, the *Fronie* was entering St. John's harbour to sell their fish, and the crew were about to indulge in one of their rewards: buying a block of ice-cream for a treat. (This was something they did only after the fish

Reg Rowe with youngest brother Ed.
Photo Submitted by Ed Rowe

Two brothers, Reg and Bill Rowe.
Photo Submitted by Ed Rowe

Reg Rowe out for a drive. Photo Submitted by Doris Rowe Wilcox

was sold). Reg wanted some of the ice-cream so badly that he took a knife and began eating the ice cream with the blade. Without realizing it, each mouthful was actually cutting his tongue! But the ice cream was so cold, and he wanted it so badly, he couldn't tell the difference between the pleasure and the pain.

Dad's brothers Eric and Reg were twins. When they were eleven years old, their father separated them by taking Reg to Labrador for the fishery and leaving Eric home. Dad told me he did not know why this happened, but Eric went to Labrador the following year. Perhaps he only had room for one of them and Reg was already showing his skill as a promising splitter.

That year the fishing was good. When the catch was ready to be sold, the *Fronie* took it to St. John's. My grandfather paid Eric and Reg a small fee that was not as much as men's wages. Nonetheless, each of them wanted something to show that they were fishing that summer. Thirty minutes after they had the money, they each came back with a pair of boxing gloves. These were not just for fun; they took the sport very seriously. When they put on the gloves, they acted like they were in a real boxing ring. This sport was something new for Chance Cove. Most people had never seen a local boxer. As it happened, both of the boys became quite good at boxing and sometimes put on a show at one of the local "times" (a community event). Others would sometimes join them in the ring – if they were brave enough to take a beating.

This continued for the two teenagers until their sixteenth or seventeenth birthday. Shortly after, Reg got a job with the Department of Education, and then he joined the Air Force. He continued his boxing after he left the Air

Force and went to work for IBM. In fact, he actually turned professional and won many trophies. After Reg left home, Eric stayed around Chance Cove for a while. Once he got his license, he drove trucks for a living. Later, he went to work for the Newfoundland Provincial Government where he worked his way up to Director of Purchasing.

The last fall that the family owned the *Fronie Myrtle*, Eric and Max went with their father and crew to Harbour Grace, where the schooner was in dry-dock. They were checking for damage that occurred on another trip. Eric and Max sailed as crewmen and the *Fronie* and crew were there a week. Food was not plentiful, so Eric and his cousin would shoot gulls, bring them aboard, pluck the feathers, and cook them as meat. Max could not eat them, but the boys seemed to think they were fine.

Max was fourteen at the time and became friendly with the locals who were his age. As there was nothing else to do while waiting, they played around with the local boys. Although Max was younger, by this time he had outgrown Eric in stature. On the last evening they were in Harbour Grace, those local fellows got somewhat nasty. Crewmen who were watching from another schooner started cheering Max on, so naturally he had to do something about it. He lunged into one fellow, and just as it got going his father, Will, came up from the schooner and saw what was going on. Will grabbed Max by the neck and put him down the forecastle of the *Fronie*.

This did not sit well with the local fellows ashore. They wanted to get even with the boys on the schooner. About eleven o'clock on the morning of the last day, three or four of those fellows came down around the schooner. What they did not know, however, was that Eric was a real boxer. When the biggest fellow started at him first, Eric soon showed his fighting skills. The first fellow made a few swings before Eric knocked him off his feet onto the wharf. Another fellow came at Eric, and he knocked him down on the wharf, too. The rest then ran off. In the meantime, the men on the other schooners were going wild.

Luckily, by the time my grandfather (the Skipper) came on the scene and said, "We are getting ready to cast off," the situation had calmed down. Will had no idea about the fighting. When the *Fronie* pulled away from the wharf, several of the local boys threw sticks and rocks. The Skipper could not figure out what the heck was going on. No one said a word. They just kept on sailing.

Ambrose Rowe was sort of an orphan. His mother died in 1935 when he was only 12 years old and left his father (Albert Rowe) with ten children to care for. Even though his father remarried, Ambrose went to live with his uncle Samuel Rowe. During this time, Ambrose sailed on the *Fronie Myrtle* for a season or two. By all accounts, Ambrose was a bit of a rough character, although he had a good heart and meant well. When Ambrose was old enough, he joined the navy and eventually they stationed him in England, where he made his home. To the best of my knowledge, Ambrose never returned to Newfoundland. He lived from December 5, 1923, until October 14, 1986.

Eric Rowe. Photo Submitted by Alicia Rowe

Max Rowe. Photo Submitted by S. Wheeler

A young Bill Rowe in the navy. Photo Submitted by Ed Rowe

Max Rowe with his youngest brother Ed in one of the early trucks. Photo Submitted by Ed Rowe

Max Rowe as a boy often accompanied his father on short trips to St. John's for supplies.
Photo Submitted by Ed Rowe

Bram Brace helped to build the *Fronie* and was a crewman for a number of years. Photo Submitted by Ed Rowe

Gordon Brace, a powerful woodsman, also helped to build the *Fronie* and sailed on her for a few years. Photo Submitted by Lulu Brace

A much older Jacob F. Smith.
Photo Submitted by Ed Rowe

Jacob F. Smith was the cook, but he liked to take over the sailing sometimes.
Photo Submitted by Jake Smith

Life on Board the *Fronie Myrtle*

Each season the crew and a cook were hired according to the availability of the men in the area. Many of them worked in the woods as loggers when they weren't fishing. Some years they chose to continue logging. From season to season, the crew of the *Fronie Myrtle* varied, but they all had to adjust to tough living conditions on board the schooner. The staples were hard bread, beans, sugar, flour, tea, molasses, salt beef, butter, lard, salt, baking soda, potatoes, onions, and anything they could catch on their voyage. The schooner also carried dried fruit such as raisins, and prunes, but apricots were a luxury. Baked or boiled beans were part of every meal. The cook made bread almost every day, and the treat on Sunday for the crew was a breakfast of fish and brewis. To wash it all down, the schooner carried two forty-five gallon wooden barrels of fresh water.

Inside the schooner, there were seven bunks, two in a cabin in the back of the ship and five in the forecastle. In the galley, there was a small table with a wooden ledge along the sides to keep the dishes from rolling off in high seas, a wood stove for cooking, and a small pantry to store the food provisions. The sleeping quarters and eating room were all crammed into one small space, so the crew had to make the best use of every inch of the schooner. The forecastle definitely had an odd shape. It was fashioned like the front of the boat: about eighteen feet long and the width of the bow of the schooner. The foremast came right down through the deck. A table ran up in the centre of the room with its wide end attached to the foremast. That side of the table was about three feet wide and came to a pointed end towards the front of the boat. Benches lined each side of the table.

A six-foot ladder was used to enter or exit the forecastle. To the left of the ladder was the small wood-burning stove with a rail around the top. The stove area took up about three square feet. On the same side were two bunks close to the ceiling, end to end. On the other side, across from the stove, was a cupboard that took up about three square feet of space from floor to ceiling. This is where the hard bread, prunes, dried apricot, beans, and flour was stored. To prevent any accidents or spillage, there were no cans or bottles in that storage space. There were three bunks on this other side: two were end-to-end and one was under the bunk closest to the cupboard.

This space might seem small for seven men, but most of them were less than six foot in height. Besides, when they were in the forecastle, they were either sitting at the table or lying in their bunks. Most of the time they were up on deck or out in the ocean with the nets and other gear. If you were not a smoker, it hardly mattered. There was a constant haze and the ever-present smell of Beaver tobacco in the forecastle.

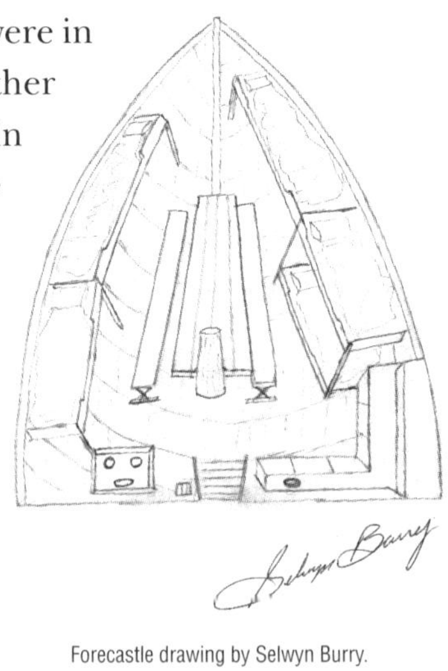

Forecastle drawing by Selwyn Burry.

Riding the Waves

If there was not much spring ice, the first trip for the *Fronie Myrtle* would usually be a voyage in May to St. John's carrying such items as wood, splits, hoops, and railway ties. The schooner would tie up to the wharf if there was room. Otherwise she would anchor along the south side of the harbour in company with a number of other schooners. The *Fronie* would stay there about a week and then return from St. John's with supplies for small businesses: coal, beef, pork, flour, and lots of salt for the fishermen.

There would be supplies for other communities, too. The *Fronie* sailed to places such as Greens Harbour, Bellevue, Sunnyside, Deer Harbour, St. Jones Within, and Little Heart's Ease. All these places had good harbours where the schooner could anchor for a day or two to unload. The supplies were carried from the ship using the motor-boat, which the men also called a skiff. Towed behind the schooner, it measured roughly 26 feet in length and had a small gas engine called a "make-and-brake" motor. The engine had one cylinder and a small battery big enough to hold a charge to ignite the gas. In the case where a schooner did not have its own motor power, the skiff towed the schooner inside the harbour to its anchoring position.

One time the *Fronie Myrtle* came to Chance Cove with a load of coal for the two schools. It was late in the evening when they arrived and they were unloading the coal by motor-boat. My dad, Max, fell off the motor-boat into the salt water. He swam around for a while in the icy water until someone hauled him aboard the skiff. That night there was a "time" to open up the new school. Major Brown, who was on the school board, was there for the opening. My grandmother Phoebe did not want dad to go because of his experience that day in the salt water. She was afraid he might get a chill. But like any young man, dad was determined to go anyway. When everyone else prepared and went to the time, he managed to talk his mother into letting him go, too. While his father was a stern man, my dad's mother was more forgiving.

Every June, the men prepared to go to Labrador. This involved another trip to St. John's for the provisions they needed, followed by the actual trip to Labrador. At an average speed of seven knots, the trip to St. John's for supplies could be accomplished in one day. As soon as the schooner was loaded with supplies, they set sail for the coast. The trip to the fishing grounds off the Labrador coast usually took the *Fronie* one or two weeks sailing depending on the weather conditions. Some men got horribly seasick.

Ed remembers his father Will telling him about a trip across Trinity Bay when a storm came up and it was Will's turn at the steering. The wheel on the schooner was not enclosed, but it was positioned towards the stern of the boat on the open deck. Like most of the men, he chewed tobacco. As he worked away at the wad, the salt spray would go in his mouth and he had to spit out the chew of tobacco. He said it was so stormy, and Will was so agitated, he chewed a whole plug of tobacco while crossing Trinity Bay.

When she returned from Labrador in the fall, the *Fronie* made more freighting trips around the bay and into St. John's. Then, after Christmas, the men anchored the schooner in George's Cove at Rantem and tied her up securely. Some of the woodcutters who harvested sale wood and splits to sell in the spring actually used the schooner for a floating house in the winter. Sometimes six or seven men at a time stayed on her during the week and would then come home by motor-boat on the weekends. They did whatever was necessary in order to earn a meagre wage.

Sometime during the 1940's, the Newfoundland government decided to build a bridge over the small river that ran through the community of Sunnyside. A lot of sand was needed for the concrete, and it all came from Chance Cove beach. Here was another chance to put the *Fronie Myrtle* to good use. First, the fishermen in Chance Cove would load up their fishing tubs and barrels with sand from the beach. Then the barrels and tubs would be taken to the *Fronie* by motor-boat. After the tricky exercise of hoisting those barrels and tubs on board, the *Fronie* delivered the sand to Sunnyside. The fishermen were paid according to the size and number of tubs they delivered. This extra cash supplemented their earnings for the coming months.

Technical Matters

When the hull of the *Fronie Myrtle* needed painting, the Skipper waited until there were a few days of fine weather with no wind. Then he and some of the crew would moor the schooner in the cove by the Point. They attached ropes from the shore to one side of the ship and then to the motor-boats. The skiffs then pulled the *Fronie* over on her side until she was barely out of the water. This exposed one complete portion of the hull. After they let the hull dry completely, they painted it. When the paint dried, they slackened the ropes and put her back in the water. They repeated the process for the other side. It was quite a production and had to be done with great skill. If any of the tackle broke, the work would be wasted. More important, some of the men could have been seriously injured.

Navigating a schooner ship and knowing the speed of the ship and where you were headed were skills that my grandfather had in spades. He did not have gadgets like the GPS and sonar that sailors use today. He used a compass, weather-glass, pocket-watch, a device they called a "log," plus a number of maps or charts for the coastal waters or, as the men on the *Fronie* called them, "sheets." And then there was always a healthy dose of common sense.

Most of the maps and charts from the ship did not survive or were given away and used on other vessels. A few of the charts are still around. Uncle Ed keeps them with the schooner's loan documents that my grandfather received from the Newfoundland Commission of Government. The documents are the ones shown in this book as well as the chart that is reproduced here. Most of the original tools used in the building of the schooner are still saved. They are in my uncle's private collection.

The following rough map indicates the most common places along the coast of Newfoundland and Labrador where the *Fronie Myrtle* stopped on her voyages. Hopedale was the farthest place they travelled on the Labrador coast for fishing. St. Anthony was a popular place to stop on the way to the Labrador fishing grounds. It was at St. Anthony where schooners replenished their provisions for the journey or made repairs to their schooners.

In 1933, the Newfoundland Government appointed the Amulree Commission to investigate Newfoundland's financial problems and to make recommendations about ways to improve the economy. The report also included a description of social, economic, and political conditions across the whole country. The commission produced a number of maps showing the electoral districts and population, religious denominations, railways and steamship routes, roads, and fishing areas around the coast.

The Newfoundland Heritage Website has given permission for me to use two of their maps from the Amulree Commission dating back to 1933. One map shows the fishing grounds off the coasts of Newfoundland and Labrador and notes the total catch of fish in each area. (The Labrador Cod Fishery quota was 320,000 quintals while the Newfoundland Shore Fishery was 700,000 quintals.) The map shows the cod, halibut, herring, and squid fishing grounds. Salmon were fished along all parts of the coast. The second map shows the coastal boat route during the period around 1933. These vessels travelled all around the Island and even went as far north as Nain on the Labrador coast. These are some of the places visited by the *Fronie* on the way to St. John's and on the way to Labrador.

Rough map of the *Fronie*'s stops.

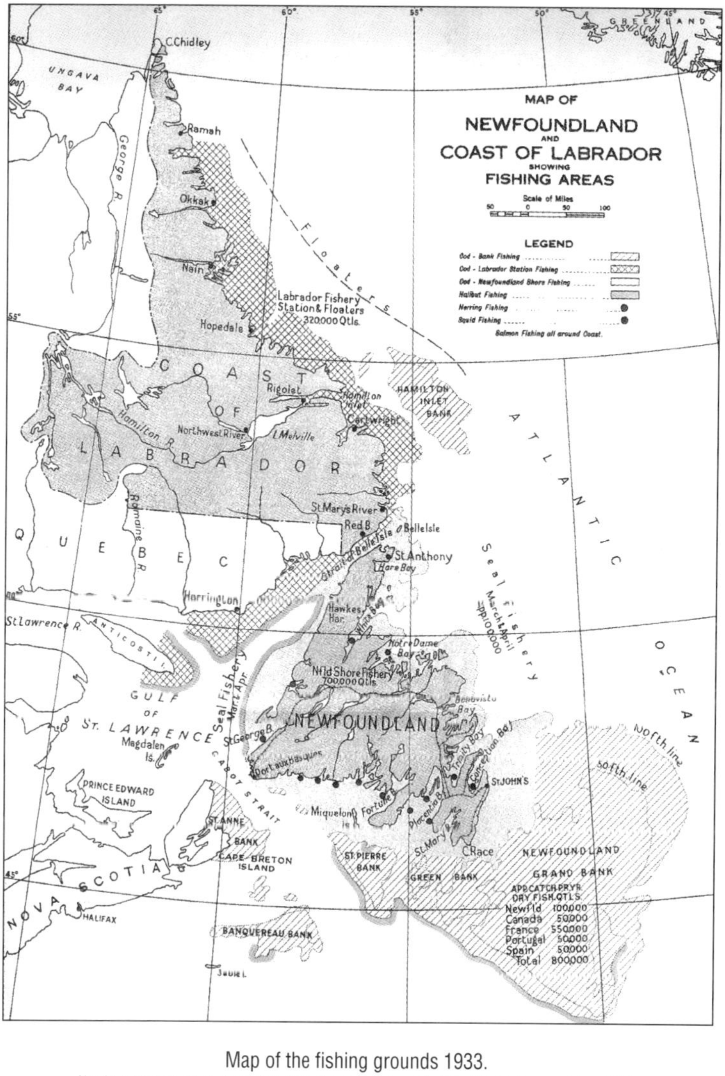

Map of the fishing grounds 1933.

Newfoundland Royal Commission 1933 Report (London: His Majesty's Stationary Office, 1934)
Reproduced courtesy of the Newfoundland and Labrador Heritage Website

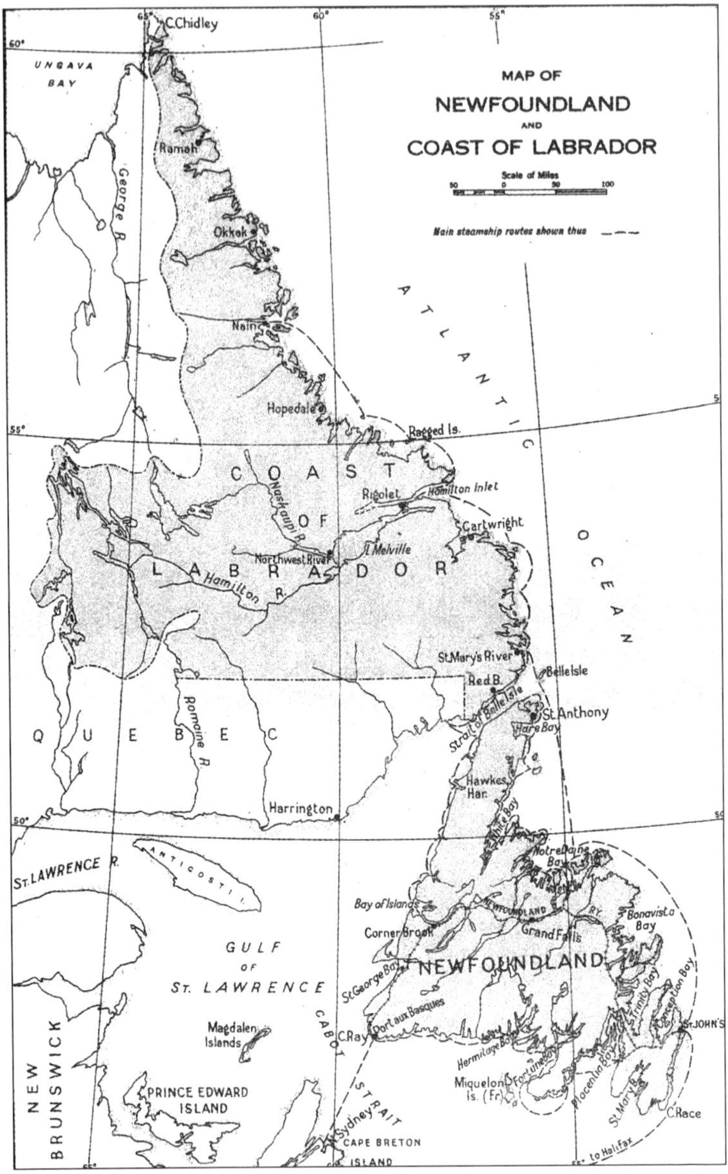

The coastal boat route 1933.

Newfoundland Royal Commission 1933 Report (London: His Majesty's Stationary Office, 1934)

Reproduced courtesy of the Newfoundland and Labrador Heritage Website

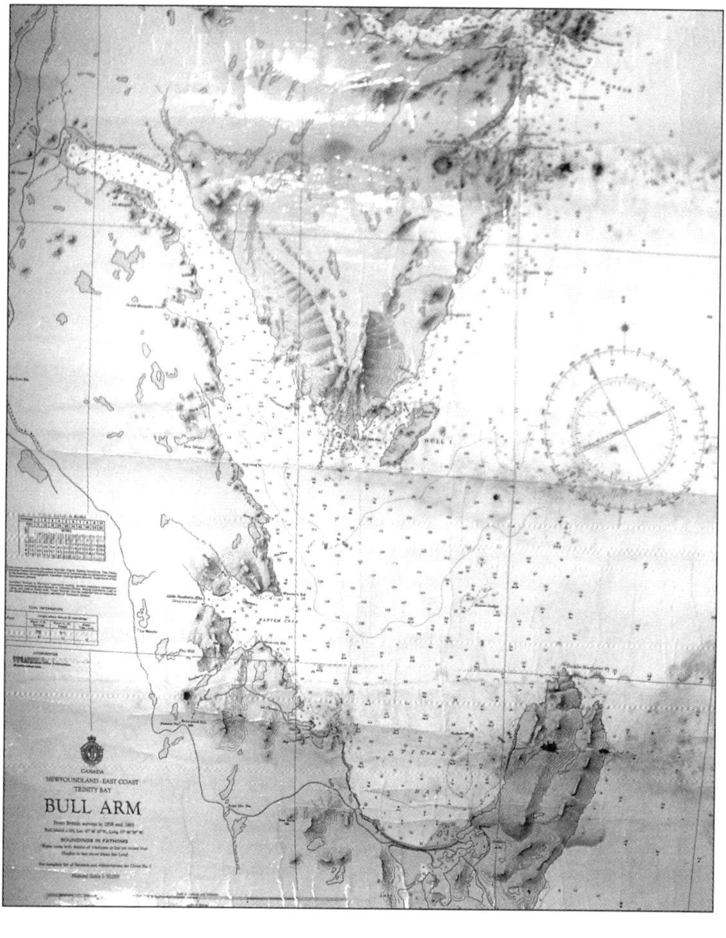

Original chart used on the *Fronie*.

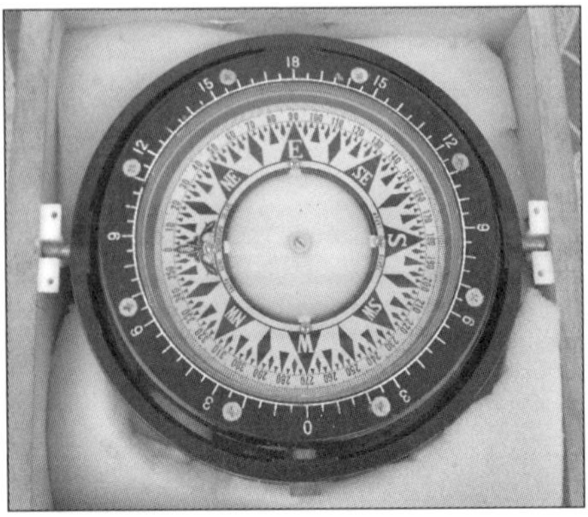

Ship's Compass: Similar to the one used on the *Fronie*. A compass is a navigation instrument, either magnetic (showing magnetic north) or gyro (showing true north).

Weather-G Glass (barometer): Measures atmospheric pressure indicating low- or high-pressure systems. This is the original used on the *Fronie*.

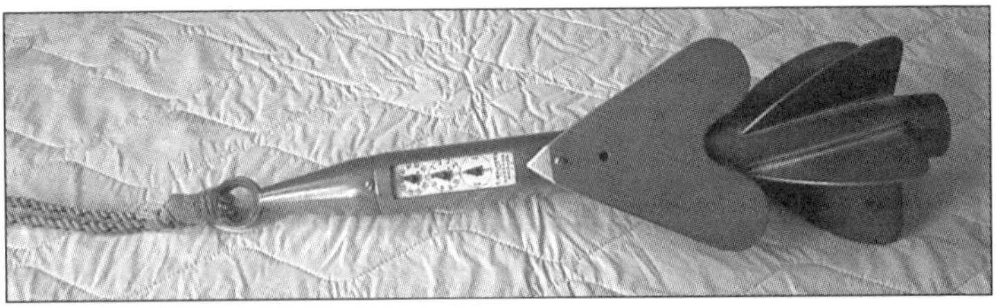

Mechanical Ships Log: Acted like a car's odometer. Dragged through the water, the tail part spun around which turned the mechanism for the dials. A pocket watch was used to note the amount of time the log was in the water. This way the skipper could calculate their speed by using the amount of time and the distance travelled.

In addition to the cod traps, the crews also used the hook-and-line method to catch the fish. However, cod traps were the most reliable – and efficient – way to catch fish. When the conditions were good, the men could haul as many as 30 to 45 quintals a day and even more. My grandfather had two cod traps, one much larger than the other. The big trap he made himself. Where the small one came from dad wasn't sure, although it is possibly Will made that one, too. Nowadays, the fishermen buy all their twine or linnet already made up. Then they knit it together to make the trap, nets, and seine.

Back in the 30's and 40's, my grandfather bought the twine and his sons helped him knit it together. Dad told me that in his mind, he could still see the pile of linnet in the corner of the room. It was long work; they had to knit some of it every night. Fortunately, dad was quite good at making nets. He told me he used a stall made from a piece of thin leather so the twine would not cut his little finger. This little device took the strain when he pulled the knot tight.

A cod trap was constructed from four walls of linnet moored with anchors or killicks to hold it square and in place. On the side towards the land, it was open in the middle so the fish could swim in. One part – called a leader – reached from the doorway in the trap towards the land. When the fish were swimming near the land, they would strike the leader made of linnet and swim by it until they came to the doorway in the trap. Then they would go right into the trap, swimming around until the fishermen came to close the doors and load the fish into the motor- boat.

It is not easy to find a killick anymore. They were an inexpensive replacement for an anchor made of iron, but very few sailors use these primitive devices anymore. In my grandfather's time, however, a killick was an inexpensive substitute for a "real" anchor. The men would cross two pieces of wood to make the claws and then attached four sticks to the claws to hold a long rock for weight. Then they tied the sticks together on top to hold the rock in place. They made these killicks in all different sizes, depending on the size of the vessel and the strength needed to hold it in place.

One old lobster fisherman from Chance Cover named Isaac Smith told dad an unusual story. He dreamt he actually *was* a killick. In the dream an old fisherman took him down and tied him to the back of his cod trap to hold it in place. That night a very strong wind from the northeast blew in on the land and the killick broke clear. Because of the heavy sea, the rock came out of the killick and the wooden frame washed upon the beach in Chance Cove.

Now there was an old woman (everyone called her Aunt Liz) in Chance Cove who would visit the beaches frequently to collect any scraps of wood that the sea brought in. She was a big woman and dad said he could picture her wearing a large white apron. Some folks used to say she could carry half a cord of wood in the apron.

Well, Ike dreamt he saw her coming down the beach and he shivered to think what was going to happen to him. When she got near him he heard her say, "My, what a nice bit of wood for baking my bread." With that, she brought her big leather boots down on him, cracking him in pieces. She gathered him in her apron and headed towards her home. She brought the pieces of killick in and stowed them near the stove. When she opened the stove door, he could see the roaring fire.

By this time Ike's wife heard the loud moaning of her husband in bed and awoke to find him kicking with his feet. She was sure he was having a heart attack.

Meanwhile, in the dream, the old woman had grabbed an armful of killick wood to put in the stove. Ike let out a blood-curdling scream and woke himself up. His wife was frightened half to death and said to him, "What in God's name were you dreaming about?"

Sailing on the Schooner

Bramwell Brace gave this oral account of the four years from 1936-1939 when he sailed on the *Fronie Myrtle*. His great-grandson Mark Bennett recorded it and transcribed it.

The crew would sail to St. John's in May to pick up provisions for their trip. This would include food items such as salt beef and pork, hard-bread, tea, sugar, flour, and prunes. They would also need salt to preserve the fish they had caught. This was measured in hogsheads (53 ½ Imperial gallons), and the ship usually took on 100 hogsheads of salt. They might also buy extra rope, twine, oil clothes, jiggers, and fuel for the skiff's engine. They would also have brought many provisions from home such as cod traps and salmon nets, splitting knives, and sharpening stones, and any line knitted during the winter. They would carry barrels of fresh water for drinking and washing (they didn't wash more than their hands and faces very often as this would waste water!). The Fronie Myrtle *had three 500-pound anchors, which were made by Mark's great-grandfather Bennett in Green's Harbour.*

They would set sail in early June. Then, if winds were favourable, they would reach the Labrador coast in one to two weeks. Under full sail, the schooner could travel at a speed of 10 knots an hour. The farthest north that Bram went was Cape Harrison. Another town that they anchored off was Battle Harbour, which was the largest community on the Labrador coast. Depending on the weather conditions, they also stopped at other towns along the shore of Newfoundland, including St. Anthony.

When they reached a fishing ground, they would launch their little skiff and set their traps. Since there were only four hours of darkness in Labrador during the summer months, they would rise at 3 a.m. to begin their busy day. First, they would go out in the skiff and haul their traps. They would bring the fish back to the schooner. All the crew would split and gut the fish and then two of them would stay back to salt the fish while the others went out to set their traps again. This process might take place five times a day before they took a little lie-down for three or four hours around 10 p.m. If the fishing was good, this would last until Sunday, when everyone rested in his bunk.

If it was too windy to haul traps, they would use their hand-lines and jiggers to fish. This catch would again be cleaned and salted. Very windy days would be spent berry-picking on the coast. When they returned home in the fall, all of their containers would be filled with bake-apples, blueberries, partridgeberries, and raspberries. They would also hunt birds for their meals.

If the fishing was good, they could return home in two-and-a-half months. However, if the fishing was slow, they could stay as long as four months. The schooner could hold up to 1000 quintals (120 pounds in a quintal) of fish. The first year the schooner sailed, they brought back 500 quintals of fish and sold it for $2.50 a quintal. Unfortunately, this was not enough to cover the mortgage and the cost of provisions, so the crew did not make any money that summer. During the war in 1939, when the price of fish went to $9.00 a quintal, the owner, William Rowe, managed to pay off the schooner and pay the crew.

After returning from Labrador, the fish was not taken to St. John's and sold immediately. First, it had to be dried on fish flakes. There was not enough room in Chance Cove to do this, so people in the communities of Deer Harbour and Little Heart's Ease would dry the fish on their flakes for twenty-five cents a quintal. Later in the fall, the fish would be collected and brought to Baine Johnson in St. John's.

My father filled in the rest of the details about the fishing process. For example, the fishing premises at Chance Cove could handle about 200 quintals of fish. Everyone helped to off-load this fish at the Rowe's stage, wash it out, and dry it on the flakes. This required a lot of hard work, especially if you struck bad weather. Usually the whole family took part in this big event.

The *Fronie* took the rest of the fish to small villages down the coast, where the crew handed it out to families who would wash and dry it for a small fee. Part of that process involved weighing out the fish and the salt according to how much they thought they could handle. When the fish was dried and ready, the schooner would pick it up and weigh it again. Dad told me he never heard his father complain about losing any fish. These people were as honest as the day is long.

One time when my grandfather settled with one old woman, he realized he owed her $10.00. When he passed it to her, she said, "I like to have a ten dollar bill as big as a schooner mainsail."

According to Bram, although the schooner's catch didn't always cover the bills and there were long hard summers of toil on the Labrador coast, the work did provide employment to a small number of people during the construction and operation. However, its main purpose was to bring all of the food and other products into the community. It was a way that the community got their provisions for the winter. The schooner also gave a feeling of pride to the men who had built the fast, seafaring ship with so few tools in such a short time. They were proud of their *Fronie Myrtle.*

Mark says that he could see a tear roll down his great-grandfather Bram's face as he said he would love again to feel the wind in his face while standing on her deck.

More Adventures on the Sea

Indian Tickle on the Labrador coast was a good place for fish. However, it had a very rough shore that made it dangerous for schooners to anchor. You not only got the wind but also a terrible swell from the ocean. One such night after the men cleaned the fish and had turned in, the wind rose to gale force with a heavy swell from the ocean. The Skipper called all the crewmen on deck. They dropped an extra anchor called the ketch anchor to aid the two already in place.

A schooner would have had two large (about 500lb) anchors in the head of the schooner. The ketch anchor would be in the back of the schooner. Normally they would drop one head anchor, but if it was windy, they would drop both. When anchored out, a schooner normally would ride head to the wind. If there was a chance that the end of the boat was going to twist around with the wind, the chain on the head anchors would twist around as well. This twisting might make the large head anchors trip, so they would drop the ketch anchor to try to hold her in place against the tide.

The *Fronie* was holding her own and the Skipper figured they were going to be okay. But such was not the case. Through the darkness, they saw another schooner drifting right down across them. Both schooners tangled together for a brief time. Things did not look too promising and crewmen were scurrying around trying to free the other schooner. The tangling together had caused the two schooners to drag their anchors, so both schooners were now drifting. With a tremendous effort, the crew finally separated the two schooners. The *Fronie Myrtle*, with the extra anchor out, held her mooring until the storm passed.

My uncle Reg was twelve years old at the time, and he told my dad he would never forget that night. He had made his uncle Sam promise to help him aboard the skiff if they had to abandon the schooner. The next morning they saw the schooner that had tangled with them the night before, plus three or four others – all on the beach. Their entire catch was scattered along the shore, and all hopes for a successful year were gone.

My dad's cousin Walter Peach from Red Harbour, Placentia Bay, also sailed on the *Fronie Myrtle*. When he returned from Labrador, he had many stories to tell. On one trip, for example, they were crossing the straits just before dark so they decided to go in St. Anthony for the night. Many schooners did this for needed supplies and because it was a good harbour to moor the schooner. The wind was blowing quite hard and the *Fronie* was sailing at full sail with a bumper load of fish. My grandfather did not slack anything; he sailed right up between the other schooners, hove to, and dropped the anchor.

No sooner had they dropped anchor when another schooner pulled up to the side of the *Fronie*. Two or three men from the schooner enquired about the *Fronie*, who they were, and where they were heading. The Skipper said to my grandfather, "Over the years I've seen schooners come in here and I've seen schooners leave, but I never seen anything like that before." He said she was going like a "flame of sculpins." This made the crew from the *Fronie Myrtle* feel very proud.

The second summer my uncle Reg went to Labrador he was twelve years old, and by this time he had accomplished the art of splitting fish. So he often gave my grandfather a hand on board the *Fronie Myrtle.* The men on the schooner used to visit some of the smaller islands to kill birds for food, because that would be the only meat they had on board. It would give the men something to eat besides fish. On one visit, my uncle Reg found two young gulls and brought them back to the schooner to rear them up. He put them in a puncheon tub with a piece of net over them. When they left Labrador on their return trip, Reg decided he would bring the two gulls home before he released them. When they were coming across the straits, however, it got so rough that the two gulls actually drowned on deck before they got to St. Anthony. Sometimes it was not all smooth sailing on the *Fronie Myrtle.*

The crew of the *Fronie* usually tried to sail hard and fast and keep company with certain other schooners. One such vessel, the *John B. Miller*, belonged to a man named Adam Green. His son Wallace Green was Second Hand. Wallace was quite agile, an excellent carpenter and boat-builder. On one trip home, the *John B. Miller* left St. Anthony a half-hour before my grandfather. However, the *Fronie Myrtle* was a little faster than the *John B. Miller* and soon closed the distance. When they got close, they saw the men on the *John B. Miller* raise the topmast sail to try to get an extra push. However, no sooner was the sail in place than the top block on the mast came unhooked and fell to the deck.

As the men on the *Fronie* watched, they saw Wallace jump in the rigging and climb towards the top. The wind was quite strong with the boat listing towards port and the spray flying over the bow. This was not an easy task for Wallace, but he made it to the top and hooked the block. No sooner had he descended to the deck than the block let go again. Up the rigging went Wallace a second time. This time he made sure it was going to stay in place.

In spite of their efforts, Will's brother Sam said we still passed the *John B. Miller.*

"Some buddies," he said.

In November, 1943, the *Fronie Myrtle* and her crew were making their last trip from St. John's with the provisions for the winter in Chance Cove and places like Bellevue, Thornlea, and Sunnyside. They had come through Baccaleu Tickle sometime before dark with a fair wind from the western. They figured they would have a good time coming in Trinity Bay and would make it home by morning. This was not to be.

Sometime before midnight, the wind freshened with heavy snow-squalls. When the snow hit, my grandfather and his brother Sam planned a course of action that would take them well clear of the land so they had lots of room to manoeuvre in the open bay. They would set a course, run her off for approximately an hour, and head her back again. Snow fell heavy all night and visibility was zero. Every man was on deck trying to see through the snow. My grandfather said it was the longest night of his life.

He ran her off, then back again, and prayed they were making good judgement in what they were losing or gaining in drifting and tacking. Daylight finally came, as it always will. However, nothing could be seen: only snow and the ring of water around the boat. As it got lighter, my grandfather decided to head closer to what he thought was land. And so, with every man on lookout, he kept a straight course. After little more than an hour had passed, one of the lookouts yelled, "Hard down, hard down." My grandfather brought her around. The lookout came aft and explained that he thought he saw a hill of snow when there was a list (break) in the falling snow. My grandfather hauled her around again to head for what the man thought he saw.

Sometime later, another yell went up and he hauled her around again. But this time when my grandfather ducked for the main boom to pass over his head, he saw a crown of land not much bigger than a roof of a house. My grandfather yelled out to Sam and Little Jake to see if they saw the same thing. They replied that they had. He asked, "Did you recognize it?" They said no they had not seen it before. My grandfather said, "I think it was the crown of Copper Island." They both looked at him and said they thought he was right.

Copper Island is a small island rock approximately fifteen miles from Chance Cove. This time when he hauled her in, they came in closer and low and behold, Copper Island burst out of the snow. He hauled her around again to set a course for Chance Cove. Before they reached home, the snowstorm was over. You would think this story is over but like so many sea stories, it was far from the end.

They had reefed the sails the night before when they first entered Trinity Bay. However, they did not realize that the spray and wet snow had turned everything to ice. My grandfather ran her up near Chance Cove Island and made a tack to bring her into the cove for mooring. Because he had done this a hundred times before, he brought her in just where he wanted her. He yelled to the men to drop anchor and lower sail. However, when the anchor dug in the bottom, the block and tackles on the main sail were frozen.

My grandfather knew he was going to lose control of the schooner, so he yelled to get the anchor in quick. Immediately the sails filled with wind as the schooner turned and headed for Chance Cove point. The schooner was loaded down with cargo and a winter supply of bagged coal on deck for the two schools. As the boat was getting closer to the point, he was yelling for the men to get the anchor off the bottom. With seconds to spare, they freed the anchor and she answered the steering.

There is a white shoal bottom off the point of land at the entrance to the harbour. As they passed over it, my grandfather said he stood on his toes waiting for the bump. However, they cleared the point, pulled out from the cove in clear water, and removed the ice from the frozen tackle.

So many schooners struck nights like this and never returned. It was just as hard on the women folk, too. My grandmother Phoebe knew the time they had left St. John's by way of Gerald S. Doyle News, which broadcast at 7:45 every night. However, my grandmother could only pray and make herself believe that they reached a safe harbour before the snow came.

Ice was one of the biggest concerns for sailors aboard Newfoundland schooners. There was no easy way to spot icebergs or growlers during the fishing trips to Labrador, especially during the night or in foggy weather. On one trip to those waters, the *Fronie Myrtle* was sailing for St. Anthony when my grandfather learned that there were two big icebergs in front of the harbour. There appeared to be plenty of room between them, so the schooners were navigating through that passage. When the *Fronie* was exactly between the two icebergs and it was too late to turn back, my grandfather realized that the two bergs were actually joined underneath the water.

He had no choice but to proceed – and they made it through without any problem. To their surprise, the next morning when they left they saw that the iceberg was broken in two. My grandfather said he dreamt about those icebergs for several nights after this frightening incident.

When my dad Max was growing up, any young fellow worth his salt knew the story about Neptune. This phantom would crawl over the side of the schooner after leaving port and chase some young man who was making his first trip at sea.

Naturally, all the old hands were in on this prank and they made it look real. The person he was chasing was too frightened to know that it was a prank. The young man would be distracted while one of the crew would get this other fellow dressed. He would put on an old pair of ripped up rubber pants, a pair of grubby boots, a sweater full of holes and a cap on his head. To cover his face, he used strings of oakum. In his hand he would hold a piece of rusty iron hoop. Neptune would then chase the poor victim, all the while threatening to shave him with this nasty piece of metal. The prank was always good for many laughs.

A Sailor's Diary: Eli William Rowe, 1945

My uncle Bill (Eli William Rowe) wrote a day-by-day account of a trip that he took to The Labrador in 1945. (This was the way sailors referred to that coast at the time.) The voyage lasted from June to September, which was the longest fishing trip ever taken by the *Fronie Myrtle.* These are the entries from Eli William Rowe's diary for that daring adventure.

June 25 (11 a.m.)

We left home with the wind blowing hard from the northwest. Fortunately, we reach Deer Harbour and all is well. We have all the sails up now as the wind is dropping a little. We expect to get to Trinity, where we will make port for the night. However, while crossing Trinity Bight, we decide to go on to Catalina to make anchor for the night. We are hoping to see some more schooners bound for The Labrador, but we are disappointed.

June 26 (6 a.m.)

The wind is blowing from the west and civil. The Skipper decides to leave. In the middle of the bay, the Skipper thinks it would be better to steer course and make harbour in Bonavista Bay. Finally, schooners are sighted running out of the bay, so our course is altered again for Cabot Island. It has been civil all day and the two engines have been running continuously, trying to make the run before dark. It is beginning to get dark, the tide is running against us, visibility is poor and we have difficulty in forming the land. Because some breakers are sighted direct in our course, the order is given to hard up. We barely escape striking the rocks. The engines are stopped and the schooner is hove too. By sounding the water, we see that anchorage would be best. We talk of our escape and try to forget, which we cannot do. Tired after a hard day, we go to sleep hoping for fair winds in the morning.

June 27

The Skipper has us up this morning at the break of dawn to show us that we are in a critical place. The sails are hoisted and we try to make the run again. Soon our good ship strikes and the cry is heard, "We have struck a rock." The sails are lowered; the schooner is beginning to pound on the rocks. "My ship is doomed!" cries the Captain, and the order is given to make ready the motorboat. We are going to abandon the ship. Plank is sighted floating up; the anchor is dropped to hold the schooner when it begins to slide off the rocks. Afraid that the ship is leaking badly, we try the pumps but find that no water has entered the ship. The ship begins to slide off the shoal, so we quickly get the anchor aboard and with the aid of the motorboat tow our ship to safety. Talking of our ship's narrow escape, we begin to prepare for a hasty voyage to St. Anthony, where our schooner can be dry-docked, repaired, and we will then continue our voyage to The Labrador.

June 28

This is early in the morning and we will soon reach the French Shore. We were at sea all night, making all the speed we can for St. Anthony. It's been very civil with no wind. The engines have been running continuously since we left Catalina, and forcing them so much has caused one to break. We are now left with only one engine and no wind. We are beginning to feel the effects of only getting very little sleep.

St. Anthony is now in sight. We hope we have a short time waiting to get on dock, but luck is once again against us. There are several schooners ahead of us. In port, we are kept busy for a while; one of the schooners has a bad leak, so we lend a hand to help move the cargo of salt.

June 29

After putting our schooner underway and through another test, we find she is not leaking so bad. Now I believe that our luck is changing, for when we enquire we find that our engine can be fixed within a day. This will solve some of our problems. The First Engineer and myself, the only two unmarried men aboard, are disappointed in the girls of this beautiful settlement, for we think they are not so nice-looking as the girls we have left behind in our own small town.

June 30

When we receive reports from the steamer, we find there have not been any fish on The Labrador so far. That makes us think we will not be too late for the fish. Still testing our schooner, we are glad to learn that the leak is not very bad. Now we are thinking of going on without waiting to get docked, which will take us another week. There are schooners arriving here every day. We know we will have many friends who have not reached The Labrador yet. Will we get a load of fish this summer? No one can answer that yet, but we have faith and faith can load the schooner itself.

July 1

The wind is still blowing this Sunday morning from the northeast and very cool. There are not many attractions. We are just resting and enjoying the Sabbath Day. The girls of this port are not very friendly to sailors, so we do not think much of them. After tea, the church looks inviting, and the remainder of the day is spent in worshipping at The Salvation Army.

July 2

The wind has changed and is blowing from the southwest. Now there are signs of it freshening to a moderate breeze. Schooners are preparing to leave, so we make haste to be on our way as soon as possible. The Skipper decides to push across the Straits, steering for The Labrador. Halfway across the straits, cork is sighted floating on the water and is thought to be a salmon net. After the order is given to hard down, the schooner is brought around to try to pick up the net. A grapnel is made fast and hove into the net. However, owing to the wind, our attempt is a failure. We are on our way again minus a grapnel and bolt hook. After a long run, we reach Sizes Harbour, where we anchor for the night satisfied with knowing that we are on the Labrador Coast.

July 3

We are awakened once again very early, although our skipper is not so anxious to leave. The barometer is dropping fast, and we know a storm is approaching. The other schooners are preparing to leave. We prepare to sail, knowing that if a storm does come on we can make harbour almost anywhere along the coast. It's very calm and the engines are running. Soon the wind comes from the northwest, and this aids us in passing four of the schooners that were before us. Reaching Snug Harbour, the wind veers to the northeast forcing us to make harbour. Finally the wind abates somewhat as we push on again to try to get through the run. Hoisting the anchor, the bosun meets an accident cutting his hand. This will make him a sick man for a while. Forcing our way through the run against the strong tide, we again meet bad luck by breaking our small engine. We are successful, however, in making Hills Harbour just as the storm comes on a combination of wind and rain.

July 4

The wind is blowing a hard breeze from the northwest. Two more schooners have arrived here during the night, and we are all waiting for the wind to change. At three o'clock, the Mate and myself go ashore to try to get a meal of birds – but we have no luck. Returning to the schooner, we find that the Engineer has been successful in getting a part for our engine. We pass the remainder of the day repairing it. Now we are ready to begin our voyage again.

July 5

The working of engines breaks our rest and we are soon on our way to try to reach our destination. When we pass all the schooners ahead of us again today, we take the lead. There has not been much wind all morning. Now a slight breeze is coming from the southwest. This is a fair wind, and we reach Grady where we are hoping to stay for a while. There is a sign of fish here, so we mark a place for our trap when the fish strikes. We sit the sweep at Penguin Island and hope that a good voyage will be taken from this berth. On our way in, we try with the jigger. Reg is the lucky man in getting the first fish for the summer.

July 6

The sign of fish is increasing, and our wish is that we will get plenty of it and be among the lucky schooners. During the evening, we visit the Marconi Pole, where we send a message home. Returning we hear news of a haul of six barrels of fish. This builds our hopes of a good voyage.

July 7

The wind is blowing from the south. It's raining hard and we are taking a spell. At noon the Mate, Engineer, and myself leave for a meal of birds. We have the good luck of killing three penguins, the first since we left home.

July 8

This is Sunday. It is a grand day the sun is shining very hot. It is the first real warm day we have had this summer. There are only two girls here in Marconi Pole, and the Engineer and myself have the good luck of meeting them today. There is not much doing, so we rest again trying to be ready when the fish comes.

July 9

The Skipper is anxious to make an early start this morning, so we quickly make ready the trap and set it. At noon, we haul but do not have any great quantity of fish. We haul again at six p.m. We are again disappointed, only getting about two barrels.

July 10

It is still holding fine and not much wind. At six a.m., we haul but the water is very dirty and the fish is more than scarce. We have tried our luck three times today, but the fish is not very plentiful.

July 11

This morning when we haul, the water seems to be dirtier than before and the fish is still scarce. The skipper is preparing to leave after breakfast. However, when we return to the schooner, the barometer is falling rapidly and it is thought that a storm is approaching. At noon, the sign of fish is a little better and we are thinking of not having to leave for a while.

July 12

There is a hard breeze blowing from the northwest, although the schooner is riding easily at anchor. The sun is shining brightly. In the morning, our work is making another piece of leader for our trap. In the afternoon, we do not do anything but take it easy.

July 13

The wind has not dropped any grêat deal during the night. It is still blowing from the northeast. At about ten a.m., we take our leader ashore to try to beat some of the dirt out of it. After spreading the leader, we are fortunate in getting close to a duck. The Skipper catches it in his hands and kills it. During the evening, the wind abates. We set the trap again with the hope of getting some fish. Returning to the schooner, the Skipper shows us some more of his keen marksmanship by killing three penguins, two with one shot. At seven p.m., we haul our trap but get only a barrel of fish.

July 14

We roll out of our bunks at six a.m. The trap is once again hauled. This time the sign of fish is a little better. We get four barrels. After doing this fishing, we go to Long Island where the fish is also scarce. On our way home, we haul again with the result of getting eight barrels. We are in hopes of getting a better haul in the evening. During the evening, the steamer arrives with the report that there is a good sign of fish further down the shore. Late in the evening, we haul again but have only two barrels. We are now preparing to leave Monday if there is no great lot of fish around at that time.

July 15

This is Sunday again and we do not have any great amount of fish yet. It is very foggy today with very little wind. There is not much doing today by anyone. We just read some books and sleep, dreaming of plenty of fish next week.

July 16

Hauling the trap this morning we get about nine barrels of fish. This cheers our spirits somewhat, and we now think that the fish is beginning to strike. At noon, we get ten barrels. After returning to the schooner, one small trap is ready. In a short time, we have it set with the hope of getting a good trip of fish from the two traps in the morning.

July 17

We are disappointed this morning – the fish is very scarce. We get only three barrels out of the two traps. This really disappoints us, and we take up our small trap and prepare to leave.

July 18

We are prepared to make this haul our last one here. So when we reach the trap, we make no delay but haul it aboard. While we are taking up the trap, the wind begins to blow from the northeast. This wind makes it impossible for us to leave today, so we will have to wait until tomorrow. During the evening, we receive word from the operator that there is plenty of fish at Smokey. Now we are hoping to make this our next port of call.

July 19

The Skipper is prepared to make an early start this morning, so we are at it bright and early. Skipper Bill Smith in the "Exotic" *is also preparing to leave. We are hung up somewhat because we have to take up some of the moorings. We are all glad to get to sea once again and happy when the sails are hoisted. Passing Packs Harbour, the Skipper thinks it would be a good idea to send the motor-boat in to find out if there is any fish. After the motor-boat returns, the Skipper decides it would be best to go to Packs Harbour for the night. It would now be too late to reach Smokey before dark.*

July 20

The wind is blowing from the southwest too much to leave and go down the shore. The fish is very scarce here this morning. This is after dinner and the wind has now changed and blowing from the northwest with rain showers.

July 21

A hard breeze is still blowing from the northwest. The Engineer and I help Mark Green to take up his trap. In the evening, we go birding and kill three divers.

July 22

This is Sunday again – a beautiful day with the wind blowing from the southeast and very warm! At two o'clock, we go ashore to try our luck with the girls. We find that they are nice-looking and friendly, but they have boyfriends. The day is quickly spent and we turn in with the hope that we will be leaving this place soon.

July 23

Again, we are disappointed. The wind is blowing from the northwest, and we cannot lie down the shore. So we have to wait for another day. At eleven o'clock, the Skipper and others go to Fish Harbour, where we hope they will hear about fish. There are three girls here cooking in schooners. We are not shy in joking with these girls and forgetting our troubles for a while. It is seven o'clock when the skipper returns with news that there is not any fish anywhere this side of Gross Water Bay. Now we do not know what to do.

July 24

The skipper is puzzled about the lack of fish. We wait to see if Mr. Green had any fish in his trap. Hearing that he never had any, we once again prepare to leave in company with the "D.V. Guy."

The wind is southeast and a grand time along. The "Fronie" *shows us some more of her sailing beauty by passing and staying ahead of the* "Guy." *We anchor in Indian Harbour with the hope of hearing news of fish somewhere along the shore.*

July 25

During the little time left last evening and this morning we have been around to the different places, but the news still is no fish. We are glad, however, when we hear there is a message at the Pole for us. Happily, we receive the news that everyone is well at home. To hear that there is no fish around anywhere has greatly discouraged us, for we were in hopes of making a good voyage. The only thing left for us to do now is to try with the jigger and trawls until we pick up a load.

July 26

This morning we get down to business right away. Striking the fish, we jig six barrels. After jigging this fish, we put out our trap, but there is too much tide and our attempt is a failure. In the evening, we jig three more barrels and this makes us feel a little better.

July 27

Everyone is expecting a load of fish, but there is still too much tide and we have to take up our trap. The fish is scarce with the jigger today. We only jig two barrels.

July 28

We try the policeman fishing gear again today and jig nine-and-a-half barrels in the morning. After dinner, we try our luck with the trap and put out the big one. Scrapping with the jigger, we jig two-and-a-half barrels.

July 29

This is Sunday, the day of rest. What can a person do today in a place like this? We try to pass the day as reverently as possible. The wind is blowing from the southwest, the sun is shining, and it's a beautiful day.

July 30

It is a very civil day, with the wind blowing from the southwest. There has been good jigging today, with about fourteen barrels.

July 31

The fish is a little scarcer today. There are five schooners here now and they are still coming. We jig eleven barrels.

August 1

The fish is still decreasing, so we have to be satisfied with six barrels. The wind is still blowing from the southwest.

August 2

It is very calm today. We have our herring net out now and we got a few this morning. The codfish is more plentiful today. We get ten more barrels to go towards the flour barrel and a winter with food for all.

August 3

The time is still advancing. I am afraid we are now in poor hopes of getting a good voyage of fish. The wind is blowing from the southwest. It is a beautiful day, but the fish is still scarce.

August 4

Awaking this morning, we are glad to hear there are several letters aboard another schooner for us from home. The letters brings us news that everyone is well at home. The wind is blowing from the south. We have a little fish in the trap and we jig a little.

August 5

Sunday again. After a hard week, we are taking advantage of it. This is a cool day; the wind is blowing a gale from the north. We pass the afternoon writing some letters home.

August 6

With the news that there is some fish at Cape Harrison, we do not know what is best to do. Some schooners are leaving today for Cape Harrison. There is no fish at all today in the trap; this greatly discourages us.

August 7

The fish is still scarce, so we are now beginning to think it would be better if we went to Cape Harrison. We do not jig any fish today and there is not any in the trap. In the evening, we take up our trap and prepare to leave tomorrow.

August 8

We try once more this morning, but there still is no fish. Now we truly ready to leave. Taking up the herring net, we bring our small trap aboard and stow it down the hole. Then we hoist up one of our anchors; this is as far as we get. There are black clouds rising up to the north, the sure sign of a squall from the northeast. This stops us again. After a while the wind and rain comes, but not as bad as we were thinking it would be.

[On August 6 and 9 of 1945, the Allied Forces dropped atomic bombs on Japan, ending World War II. It was August 13, on the way home from Labrador, when the news reached the schooner. Bill referred to August 13 in his diary as "Black Monday."]

August 9

The wind is blowing again from the northeast. Now we know that we are not likely to leave at all. In the afternoon, the wind abates a little and we jig a small amount of fish. We also put out our herring net again. We hear there is plenty of bait at Emily but no fish, so if we cannot get any bait here we will be going to Emily.

August 10

There is not any bait this morning. We jig six barrels of fish today during this calm day. It is raining now, the first hard rain for the summer.

August 11

There is poor weather now for fishing. The wind is blowing a breeze today from the west, and it does not abate before noon. Today we jig two barrels of fish, pick some bake-apples and kill some birds for our dinner tomorrow.

August 12

There is a slight breeze today. The sun is shining and it is grand to be alive. We are not working today, but resting and praying for more fish next week.

August 13

"Black Monday!' "This is a wet day, but the fish are not as scarce as usual. The bait is also not so scarce and we have a few herring. This is a calm but rainy day. When we reach the schooner, we are all wet but we have about ten barrels of fish. This cheers us up.

August 14

As usual, we are up again this morning bright and early. It is foggy and wet. Hauling our net, we have some herring and we prepare to try our trawls. After being out a little while, the wind comes from the north. So, after getting five barrels, we are forced to return to the schooner.

August 15

We are having a hurricane wind blowing from the southeast. Nobody is going fishing today.

August 16

There is no fish today and nothing to do. With the wind still blowing a strong breeze, we are forced to stay in.

August 17

We have plenty of bait today, but the wind is still blowing hard and we cannot go fishing again today. When we try our luck at berry-picking, we get three-and-a-half gallons. There are two schooners here, the first to go up loaded. They have been here all the week waiting for good sailing weather.

August 18

Saturday, the last day of the week. It is civil and a grand day for fishing. Since we have a lot of bait today, we get right down to fishing. When we finish this evening we are satisfied with twelve barrels.

August 19

The cook was busy last night, so he never had time to prepare his fish and brewis for breakfast. This disappoints us and some of us sleep in, the first time this summer. I am expecting a letter from home, but I am disappointed when the Operator informs me he has not received one.

August 20

The beginning of another week. The bait is plentiful again and we have all day fishing. The fish is not too scarce, one cannot complain. We get about seventeen barrels.

August 21

There are signs this morning of this being a poor day. The barometer is down on twenty-eight. We go fishing, but we expect the wind every minute. Soon it strikes from the northwest and we reach the schooner with three-and-a-half barrels. The bait is plentiful, so we hook up the rest of our lines. After this, we go berry-picking. We pick about three gallons. Returning to the schooner, we are glad to find that the steamer has passed and left letters for us. Reading my mail I find that my Uncle is home from Canada, after being gone for fifteen years. Also, my cousin is home from the Royal Artillery, after being gone for five years. We have no chance of seeing either of them before they go back again.

August 22

The middle of the week. This is a miserable day – wet and not very warm. The wind is blowing a civil breeze from the northeast. We are lucky with the fish today, getting about eleven barrels.

August 23

There are signs this morning of this being another wet day, but we are glad to see that after a while the wind clears up and it is a good day for fishing. The fish is scarce now with the jigger, but we get plenty of bait and we can use our trawls steadily. We do well again today, getting a lot of big fish, amounting to twelve and a half barrels. While we are doing our fish, the steamer blows at "Emily" a short distance away. Some of us stop and write several letters home, to let them know we are all well.

August 24

There is no bait today and we are very scarce of wood. Some of our crew, with several of Skipper Drodges' men, go to Pottle Bay for wood. Three of us go fishing and we get five tubs. This is a help because every quintal counts.

August 25

Soon we will get a rest from a busy week. The bait is scarce again this morning and a gale wind is blowing from the west. This week it was impossible for us to do good fishing. There are schooners passing us all the time. Some are loaded but not very many. There are quite a number passing us this morning. We are anxious to get enough berries to carry home, so we leave again this morning for more berries. We get enough to fill everything we have aboard. My brother and myself have about ten gallons, some packed in coke bottles.

August 26

We do not sleep in this morning. The cook has fish and brewis. This is a fine day. The wind is blowing a little breeze from the northeast. We sleep today as usual. Pray and hope for more fish next week.

August 27

The bait is scarce this morning, and no bait often means no fish. It is foggy with a slight breeze from the northeast. In spite of the bait, we get about eight tubs.

August 28

There is still no bait, which is beginning to discourage us for there is not any fish with the jigger. Bait is the only solution. We are at it all day, trying to scrape as much as we can and we end up with two barrels. The wind is blowing from the south. With a bit of luck, we may expect herring in the morning.

August 29

Everyone was expecting bait this morning, but there was none. Now we see that it isn't any good to stay here, so today we prepare to leave. There is plenty of crushed shell here, which we will carry home for the hens. The foxes are numerous and we have some fun this morning chasing them, almost catching one young one. We make everything ready to leave tomorrow if there is good sailing weather.

August 30

We soon have our schooner under way. The wind is about west. There are ten schooners in this fleet. The "Fronie" *shows us more of her sailing beauty by being the leader again today. We are hoping there will be fish at Grady so that we can get another hundred quintals, but we are disappointed. After getting our cask of oil that we lent* "Charley Bird," *we get underway again. Reaching Indian Tickle, the wind veers down and we anchor for the night. After being anchored for a while, the wind veers up again, so we leave and anchor at Domino.*

August 31

This is another civil morning, so we leave early to try to make another good run. We pass all the schooners again and go ahead. Before we reach American Tickles, our small engine gives out leaving us with just one engine. The Engineer gets to work. He runs new bearings into the piston leg and by twelve o'clock we have her going again. This accident brings us a long way behind the head schooner. We were hoping to reach Francis Bight for the night, but we are forced to make anchorage at Ship Harbour.

September 1

Saturday, the beginning of another day, and we have not reached home yet. We are up and at it early this morning, rolling out at two o'clock. The wind is blowing from the northwest, which means a grand time up the shore and across the straits. Reaching Belle Isle, the wind drops and veers from the southwest making us trim our sails to make St. Anthony. We reach St. Anthony at 6:30 p.m.

September 2

We were hoping to have the pleasure of spending our Sunday in St. Anthony and now we can do so. This is a good day; the wind is blowing from the south with occasional rain showers. The officer in charge of the Salvation Army here is Captain Pritchett, who spent two years at Chance Cove. We enjoy ourselves by attending the Army after tea.

September 3

The wind has changed quite a lot since last night. Now it is blowing from the northeast. If it were not foggy, this would be a nice day sailing. There is only one schooner here with us and we do not know them. At 11 a.m. we leave to try to get up the shore for a straight run across the Bay. Passing Hare Bay, the wind comes from the west and increases to a gale. We have to shorten sail, and this is exciting. After single reefing the main sail, the foresheet breaks and we have to haul the fore sail down as well as the outside jib. The wind is too hard on us now. We try to reach harbour in Crouse and in doing so we break the jumbo and have to haul it down. Then we use the jib. After this, we reach the harbour in safety.

September 4

The wind is still blowing a southwest gale this morning. There are plenty of squash-berries here, so pick some to carry home. We will have berries if we do not have anything else.

September 5

There is no slack in the southwest wind. In the afternoon, several of the crew go to Conche to send a telegram home, letting them know we are on our way.

September 6

We are sleepy this morning because we are up early and on our way. The wind is blowing from the northeast. This makes for good sailing. The water is very rough, but I do not get seasick. We reach the run after dark. Now the wind has veered down from the southwest, so we have to steam up through, reaching Half Way Point at one a.m.

September 7

It is raining this morning with winds blowing from the southwest. We are not up very early this morning. After we get up, we are under way again and leave for Seldom, which will bring us nearer home. There are a lot of schooners here at Seldom, but there are only two here that left Indian Harbour with us.

September 8

Schooners are leaving this morning when we get up and we soon get ready too. There is a hard breeze blowing now from the northeast. We run out four and-a-quarter miles. But the wind veers and blows hard so we have to come back, doing so in thirty-five minutes.

September 9

The wind has abated somewhat, so we try it again. Going out, we meet three more schooners but we do not know them. The water is really rough this time. Some of us are almost sick, but we hold out. After dinner, we think the wind is going to die out and it does after dark. When we reach Cape Bonavista, hauling in the bay we go to Shamblers Cove. We have shortened the distance by forty-two more miles today. We arrive early enough to go to the Army in Port Nelson. The officer in charge is Captain Williams from Tilton.

September 10

We were expecting good sailing this morning across the bay but a strong breeze is blowing from the southwest. We think this would be a grand day for a holiday, so we go to Wesleyville. The people are really friendly here and we enjoy a pleasant day.

September 11

The cook does not let us sleep in this morning. Rising early, we soon are under way and crossing the Bay. A civil breeze is blowing from the west. Engines are working steadily, but the wind is not very strong. It takes us a long time to reach Trinity Bay. This is a grand night, so we sail on reaching Deer Harbour at one a.m. This is where we are expecting to land our fish before we go home.

September 12

There is also another schooner here in Deer Harbour landing fish. However, we feel sure we will not have any trouble to land our fish as the folks here have made fish for us during past years. On visiting some people we know and after a little persuasion, they agree to accept our fish and we start to land it.

September 13

We do not rush, but we work steadily at the fish all day. We now wish we had our schooner full to land.

About fifty years after this voyage, my uncle Bill wrote some additional notes about the trip. Here are a few more things he remembers about the trip.

This was the year when we stopped in Deer Harbour on the way home to land our catch. The reason was possibly a combination of a small catch and the late returning from The Labrador. Normally, we would have gone home first and returned to offload.

Somewhere on the way home, we got the news of the atomic bomb being dropped and the war with Japan was over.

There was a girl. She was a cook on one of the schooners, sailing with her two brothers who owned it. We started our romance when we first met, somewhere on the voyage.

I had started a business course at the Mercy Convent in January prior to this trip and was returning to complete it when I returned from The Labrador. We both knew this. However, we felt our relationship would continue. I saw her in St. John's while we landed our fish, but I don't remember ever speaking to her again. Just a fleeting glance.

In the meantime, I had won some medal in shorthand, and the Sisters broadcast this during the summer several times on the radio. But I never heard of the medal until I returned to school in October.

We left St. John's sometime around the 10th of June, completely laden with decks in the water. There was a sea rolling in from the east, and I remember it would roll over one side and out the other. It was calm, so this sea never bothered us. I was deathly seasick. However, I determined that if I were going again to The Labrador, I was going to beat it. As soon as I could pull myself to my feet, I got to the wheel. There I stayed for four to five hours until I was well – no more trouble with seasickness.

Reg was with Uncle Sam, the main splitter. He had learned the art at age eleven and took over from Pop, who was considered the best.

In most ports on The Labrador frequented by fishing schooners, there were small wooden buildings fitted with wooden benches. On

Sundays, undoubtedly, there would be at least one service led by fishermen for fishermen. Uncle Sam was usually a leader, with several men from other vessels.

The Sisters were astounded at how I remembered my shorthand and typing so well after an absence of almost four months. Each night after crawling in my bunk, I would go over the shorthand characters and typewriter keyboard reaches in my head – and usually fell asleep doing so.

Jim Peddle's wife was dying with tuberculosis, so he stayed home that summer. I don't believe Little Jake was with us, although I can't remember why, The crew consisted of Pop, Uncle Sam, Reg, Uncle Albert Warren, Ernest Smith, William Smith (Billie), and myself.

Last Sailing

Approach life like a voyage on a schooner.
Enjoy the view. Explore the vessel.
Make friends with the captain. Fish a little.
And then get off when you get home.
(Max Lucado, *In the Eye of the Storm)*

In the fall of 1948, Will and a small crew sailed the *Fronie Myrtle* to Harbour Grace and put the schooner on dry-dock for a week. The bottom needed repairs from the damage caused when she ran aground on a previous trip. (Bill described this incident in his Labrador diary on June 27, 1945.) Fortunately, the damage to the keel had been minimal, so they had been able to sail in the meantime without the repair.

Putting the *Fronie* on dry-dock turned out to be more than just a decision about repairs. There was a bigger problem being faced by the Skipper and the crew. It was impossible not to notice the changes happening up and down the shore: the building of roads, with more trucks being used to transport goods. Highways opened up in communities all around Newfoundland, making transportation by water unnecessary. Even when water transportation was being used, power-boats of all sizes were taking over from sailing ships.

Meanwhile, the Labrador schooner fishery was no longer profitable due to the introduction of larger and more powerful boats such as long-liners and trawlers. A way of life had all but disappeared, and a new inshore fishery was in the making. Owners of newly-built plants bought fresh fish directly from the fishermen. Instead of shipping salt fish to market by way of schooner, plants sent fresh fish products to market by way of freezer trucks. Will saw the warning signs and knew he had to change with the times. Being a smart businessman, he made the decision to sell – and just in time. Unknown to everyone except his wife Phoebe, and possibly his brother Samuel, Will had already made up his mind to sell the *Fronie* before the start of the next fishing season.

In 1949, Will sold the *Fronie Myrtle* to the Whelan brothers from Little Hearts Ease. William Whelan was a previous owner of the schooner *Annie S. Clarke,* which he had purchased in 1945. As it happened, the Whelans only sailed the *Fronie* for one year. They made freighting trips to and from St. John's, and they probably did a few fishing trips as well. But the Whelans soon came to the same conclusion as Will: the best years for the schooner business were now behind them. As the cod fishery continued to decline along the coast of Labrador, there was no longer a need for schooners such as the *Fronie Myrtle.* After just one more season on the ocean, the proud sailing history of the schooner was over. The Whelans beached the *Fronie* in a nearby cove. Her sailing days were over.

This was a sad end to the gallant *Fronie Myrtle* and her courageous years along the coasts of Newfoundland and Labrador. For fifteen years she served her owners well. Through fog, snow-storms, rough water and icebergs, she carried them safely to Labrador, St. John's, and the many small communities in-between. Until 1966, her bow was still visible in a local cove and almost intact on the beach. But slowly the passing of time and the Newfoundland climate claimed her, as it had so many other Newfoundland schooners. Meanwhile, in keeping with the times, Will and his sons purchased a truck and stayed in business – but now on dry land.

Modern means of transportation may have replaced the beautiful tall-masted schooners, but they will always be an important and colourful part of our Newfoundland past. Schooners were not just fishing boats. They ferried people around the province, and they transported every possible kind of merchandise bought and sold at the time. Today these old Newfoundland schooners are remembered in pictures, books, small-scale replicas, and museums. They remind us how people lived and how our culture evolved.

There are modern schooners on the ocean today to carry on the proud nautical tradition. They are outfitted with the latest navigational tools and all the comforts of home. Although they have joined the ranks of the pleasure craft, however, there is no experience that can compare to standing on the deck of a schooner with the wind blowing, the sails up, and the taste of salt spray in your mouth.

During the later years of William Rowe's life, he would sometimes stand on the rocky shore gazing out to sea. I suspect he would daydream about the *Fronie Myrtle* and wish for those days again. Those dreams sustained my father, too. My hope is that the story of the *Fronie* will help to preserve my father's memories – and the adventurous spirit of all the Newfoundlanders who plied the waters in beautiful schooners like the *Fronie Myrtle.*

APPENDICES

COMMISSION OF GOVERNMENT

In reply please quote Reference Number /

Department of Natural Resources

ST. JOHN'S, NEWFOUNDLAND

December 1934.

Dear Sir:-

Enclosed herewith please find your copy of the following documents in connection with the schooner which this Department is assisting you to build:-

(a) Memorandum of Agreement.

(b) Indenture.

(c) Memorandum of Agreement.

Please acknowledge receipt of the above-mentioned documents.

Yours faithfully,

Secretary for Natural Resources.

Mr. William Rowe,

Chance Cove. T.B.

Letter to William Rowe from Secretary for Natural Resources

Memorandum of Agreement made this 17th day of December 194, BETWEEN William Rowe of Chance Cove, Trinity Bay (hereinafter called "the builder") of the one part AND the Commissioner for Natural Resources, acting on behalf of the Crown (hereinafter called "the Commissioner") of the other part

WHEREAS the Government of Newfoundland is desirous of encouraging the construction of schooners for use in the fisheries of Newfoundland;

AND WHEREAS the Commissioner has agreed with the builder to assist the said builder by means of loans or advances to build at Chance Cove Newfoundland a schooner of approximately 35 tons register, which schooner upon completion and registration is to be mortgaged to the Commissioner to secure such advances;

NOW THEREFORE the builder agrees with the Commissioner that upon the completion of the schooner and execution of the mortgage to the Commissioner, and until the said mortgage shall be paid off, the builder will during every fishing season employ or cause to be employed the said schooner throughout such season in and about fishing upon the coasts of Newfoundland or Labrador or elsewhere, and will prosecute or cause to be prosecuted the said fishery with due diligence; and that he will at the beginning of each season confer with the Commissioner and seek his advice as to the branch of the fishery in which he should engage; and will at the end of each such season furnish to the Commissioner for his information an account showing the entire expenses and earnings of the schooner and generally that he will do all in his power to see that the assistance given to him shall result in the more active prosecution of the fisheries of the country.

IN WITNESSS WHEREOF these presents have been executed by the parties the day and year first above written.

SIGNED, SEALED AND DELIVERED by Wm Rowe in the presence of:— Wm Humphries

William Rowe

SIGNED by the ~~Commissioner~~ Secretary for Natural Resources in the presence of:— V. T. Porter

[illegible]

Memorandum of Agreement

A

This Indenture, made the 17th day of December 1934, Between Wm Rowe of Chance Cove T.B.

(hereinafter called "the Builder") of the one part, **And** THE COMMISSIONER FOR NATURAL RESOURCES (hereinafter called "the Commissioner") of the other part.

WHEREAS the Builder is building at Chance Cove in Newfoundland a wooden fishing schooner of the approximate tonnage of 35 tons;

AND WHEREAS the Commissioner acting on behalf of the Crown has advanced to the Builder the sum of #350.00 dollars (the receipt whereof is hereby acknowledged) and has undertaken to make to the Builder further advances from time to time;

AND WHEREAS the Builder is desirous of giving security to the Commissioner for the said present and future advances;

NOW, THEREFORE, THESE PRESENTS as follows:

1. The Builder doth hereby assign, transfer and set over unto the Commissioner by way of security for the said sum of #350.00 dollars and such further advances as may from time to time be made to him by the Commissioner up to the completion of the said schooner, the said uncompleted schooner together with all timber and other material, gear and equipment, wherever situate, purchased for the construction and equipment of the schooner.

2. The Builder shall diligently and without any cessation during the usual working days and hours proceed with the construction of the said schooner and complete and equip the same ready for sea by the date specified in that behalf in the Agreement between the Builder and Commissioner dated the 17th day of December, 1934.

3. If the Builder shall commit any breach of the stipulation in the foregoing Clause contained ed the Commissioner shall have power to enter and seize the schooner and other chattels hereby mortgaged and to sell the same.

4. The Builder covenants with the Commissioner that he will from time to time execute and deliver to the Commissioner such further or other assurances and securities as the Commissioner may from time to time require, covering the schooner and all or any material and equipment wherever situate, purchased for her construction and equipment.

5. Provided always that if the said schooner shall be completed and ready for sea on or before the 1st day of June, 1935, and if the Builder shall as soon as the said schooner has been completed register the said schooner in the Registry of Shipping and execute a mortgage of the same to the Commissioner in accordance with the terms of an Agreement made between the parties and dated

Indenture

the 17th day of December 1934, then the Commissioner will release and discharge this mortgage.

IN WITNESS WHEREOF THESE PRESENTS HAVE been executed by the parties the day and year first above written.

SIGNED, SEALED AND DELIVERED
by Wm Rowe
in the presence of:—
Wm Humphries

William Rowe

SIGNED by the ~~Commissioner~~ Secretary for Natural Resources and the Seal of the Department of Natural Resources affixed hereto in the presence of:

Memorandum of Agreement made the 17th day of December Between THE COMMISSIONER FOR NATURAL RESOURCES, acting on behalf of the Crown, (hereinafter called "the Commissioner") of the one part And William Rowe of, Chance Cove, Trinity Bay, (hereinafter called "the builder") of the other part.

WHEREAS the builder has resolved to build a schooner for use in the fisheries of Newfoundland;

AND WHEREAS the Government of Newfoundland is desirous of encouraging such building, and has undertaken to assist the builder by means of loans or advances as hereinafter set forth;

NOW, THEREFORE, IT IS AGREED, as follows:

1. The builder shall build and equip at in Newfoundland during the calendar year commencing with the date of this Agreement a wooden fishing schooner of the following tonnage, namely:

   Approximately 35 Tons

2. The schooner shall be built according to a plan or design approved by or on behalf of the Commissioner.
3. The schooner shall be built and equipped in accordance with the requirements of Schedule B to the Shipbuilding Act, 1933, but no bounty under the said Act shall be payable in respect of the said schooner.
4. No material or equipment not of Newfoundland origin or manufacture shall be used in the construction and equipment of the said schooner, save with the permission of the Commissioner; such permission shall not be granted if material or equipment of equivalent kind and quality is obtainable in Newfoundland on reasonable terms.
5. No person other than a permanent resident in Newfoundland shall be employed in or about the construction of the schooner.
6. All materials for the construction and equipment of the schooner shall be obtained by the builder through the Commissioner, unless the builder obtains the prior written permission of the Commissioner, or of some officer acting on his behalf to obtain the same or any of them otherwise.
7. In consideration of the performance by the builder of this agreement, the Commissioner will from time to time during the building of the said schooner by way of loan or advance to the builder pay on behalf of the builder all bills for labour, materials and equipment which, in the opinion of the Commissioner, the builder is himself unable to pay; provided that all such bills shall before payment be certified by the builder and by an Inspector on behalf of the Commissioner as being fair, just and properly incurred.
8. The Builder shall, as soon as the building of the schooner is commenced, execute a chattel mortgage of the incomplete schooner together with all materials purchased for the construction or equipment thereof to the Commissioner in the form hereto annexed marked "A."
9. The Commissioner shall during the construction of the schooner keep the schooner, together with all materials purchased for the construction or equipment thereof, insured against fire in some good and reputable insurance office or offices; the amount of insurance being increased progressively as construction proceeds so as at all times to be sufficient to cover

Memorandum of Agreement

the value of the schooner and materials with a surplus of ten per centum. All policies shall be taken out in the name of the Commissioner; and the cost thereof shall be considered to be part of the advances to the builder under this agreement, to be covered by the mortgage and supplementary deed under Clause 11 hereof.

10. The Builder shall build and equip the schooner with all due speed and diligence applying the best methods and the best workmanship within his power; and shall complete the schooner before the 1st day of June, 1935.

11. Upon the completion of the schooner the Builder shall cause the schooner to be registered and shall execute in favour of the Commissioner a mortgage in the statutory form of sixty four shares in the said schooner, to secure the amount of all moneys advanced to the Builder under this Agreement, with interest at the rate of four per cent. per annum from the date of each advance until the date of registration, and with interest at the same rate upon the whole sum from the date of registration during the continuance of the mortgage, together with a supplementary deed of covenant in the form hereto annexed marked "B"; and for the purposes of this Clause the Commissioner's calculation of the total advances to the Builder and of interest shall be conclusive.

12. The mortgage shall be for a term not exceeding six years from the date of execution; the Builder shall covenant to pay off the mortgage by equal annual instalments payable on or before the 31st day of December in each year during the continuance of the mortgage.

13. The Builder agrees that he will during the continuance of the mortgage keep the schooner in good repair and fully equipped.

14. The Builder agrees that he will not during the continuance of the mortgage sell the schooner without the permission of the Commissioner.

IN WITNESS WHEREOF these presents have been executed by the Commissioner and by the Builder the day and the year first above written.

Signed by the ~~Commissioner~~ Secretary for Natural Resources and the seal of the Department of Natural Resources affixed hereto in the presence of:

Signed, Sealed and Delivered by Wm Rowe in the presence of:

William Rowe

GLOSSARY

Anchor: A heavy device lowered from a ship, which digs into the sea bottom to keep the vessel from drifting or shifting position.

Auger: A carpenter's hand-tool used by boat-builders to bore holes in wood.

Barking the traps: The process of dipping the traps (nets) in casts of boiling water mixed with tree bark. The original twine used in the making of traps was light coloured. The barking process preserves the material and turns it a darker colour.

Barrel (as in a "barrel" of fish): A unit of measure in the British Imperial and U.S. Systems indicating a quantity of fish weighing roughly 200 pounds.

Bone in her teeth: Describes a vessel that is well underway and is throwing spray as it travels through the water.

Bulwarks (also bullworks): A solid rail along the ship's side and above the deck built to prevent men and gear from going overboard.

Burton block-and-tackle: A system of small blocks or pulleys used to tighten the ropes or cables (shrouds) of the topmasts.

Caulk: In wooden vessels, the task of filling seams in the wood with oakum and cotton using caulking irons and hammers.

Canvas: Slang for sail. Historically, all sails were made of canvas.

Chart: A map for use by navigators that indicates both the geography of the land and the depth of the water.

Compass: Navigation instrument that is either magnetic (showing magnetic north) or gyro (showing true north).

Cord: A measurement of wood logs that is 4 feet high by 4 feet wide x 8 feet long (128 cubic feet).

Culler: The person assigned to the job of grading the salt fish being sold.

Diver: A type of sea bird, usually with reference to an ocean duck.

Forecastle: The most forward compartment of a vessel.

Foremast: The mast in the forepart of a vessel, nearest the bow.

Foresail: The sail on the foremast of a schooner, or the lowest square sail on the foremast of a square-rigged vessel.

Galley: The kitchen of a ship.

Growlers: Very small but dangerous icebergs, which were hard to see from a schooner.

Head to wind: Describes the moment when the ship's bow is turned into the wind and the sails are luffing (rippling).

Hogshead: A large cask or barrel that historically referred to various weights, but typically 63 U.S. Gallons or 54 British Imperial Gallons. On the schooner it referred to the storage of salt.

Hull: The main body of the boat, not including the deck, mast or cabin.

Jib: A triangular foresail in front of the foremast.

Jigger: A traditional Newfoundland unbaited weighted hook, often designed like a small fish, used with a line to catch larger fish by giving a sharp, upward jerk.

Jumbo: Similar to a staysail (see below).

Keel: Centerline of a boat running fore and aft. Also the timber at the very bottom of the hull to which frames are attached.

Ketch anchor: Anchor located in the back of the schooner, which was used to to hold the vessel in place against the tide.

Killick: A homemade anchor usually made of a large stone set within a framework of wooden sticks.

Linnet: The material used to construct a fishing net.

Luff: The front vertical edge of the sail, which runs along the mast (see also "head to wind" above).

Lug: To carry a heavy load.

Mainmast: The tallest mast of the ship and on a schooner the mast furthest aft.

Mainsail: The sail set on the mainmast, usually the lowest square sail.

Mast: The large wooden pole used to hold up the sails.

Navigation: The art of getting a vessel safely from one port to the next.

Oakum (caulking): Tarred hemp or manila fibers used for caulking the seams of decks and sides of a wooden ship in order to make them watertight.

Oilskin: Garments worn by sailors and treated with linseed or other oils for waterproofing.

Planking: Wood boards that cover the frames outside the hull.

Policeman: A type of fishing gear made from a baited hook and line suspended from colourful floaters.

Quintal: A British weight of 112 pounds commonly used in the Newfoundland fishery.

Reef: A line of grommets (rings) running parallel to the boom line. They secure the sail to the boom in heavy weather and can decrease the sail area to make the vessel easier to handle during high winds.

Reefing: The operation of reducing a sail by taking in one or more of the reefs.

Rigging: The lines that hold up the masts and move the sails (standing and running rigging).

Sale wood: Trees cut in winter and turned into lumber for sale in the spring to St. John's and other ports.

Sheets: Charts and maps. Also the ropes and lines used to raise and lower sails.

Skiff: A small boat. Also a motor-boat.

Skipper or **Captain:** The person in charge of a vessel and legally responsible for it and its occupants.

Splitter: The person who cuts open the codfish and removes the backbone.

Stall: A leather protector worn on the fingers when making or mending nets.

Stay: A rope or wire used to secure some part of the rigging.

Staysail: A triangular sail hoisted on a stay (as between two masts).

Stern: The aft, or rear, end of a vessel

Tacking: Also known as "coming about," a sailing manoeuvre in which a vessel turns its bow and changes direction in order to take the wind from a different direction. Describes a zig-zag movement.

Time: Local term for a social function, which might include a dance, concert, church or similar event attended by everyone in a community.

Topmast: A second spar (cross-beam) carried at the top of the fore or main mast and used to fly more sail.

Topsail: Small staysail located between the foremast and mainmast.

Traps: Nets for catching codfish.

Twine: Strong thread or string made from two or more strands or yarns twisted together.

Weigh: To haul up, as in to weigh the anchor.

West Indies fish: Low-grade Newfoundland salt fish shipped to colonies such as Jamaica and Barbados as a cheap and easily preserved source of protein.

Whole sail breeze: Sufficient wind to raise all the sails.

LIST OF SCHOONERS

These are some of the schooners mentioned in the preceding pages, along with a few of their nautical statistics where available.

Anne S. Clarke, 48-ton schooner built in Glovertown, B.B. in 1922 and purchased by William Whelan of Little Hearts Ease in 1945.

Bernice, sailed approximately in the 1930's to the 1940's and skippered by William Frank Smith, Chance Cove.

Charley Bird, referenced in the 1945 anecdote, but owner and home port unknown to this author.

D.V. Guy, 32-ton schooner in use from 1930 to 1943 and skipped by Jacob Guy, Musgrave Harbour.

Exotic, 52-ton schooner registered for sailing between 1936 to 1948 and skippered by William Henry Smith, Hodges Cove.

John B. Miller, sailed approximately in the 1930's to the 1940's and skippered by Adam Green, St. Jones Without.

Melva Abbie, 18-ton schooner built in 1906, sailed until 1914 when she was lost at Northern Bay. Schooner operated by Will Rowe's uncle Samuel Rowe and sometimes skippered by Eli Rowe (Will's father), Chance Cove.

ACKNOWLEDGEMENTS

A special thanks to uncle Edmund Rowe of Chance Cover for preserving and sharing historical documents, photographs, and uncle Bill's diary. He and his grandson Mark Bennett also shared Bram Brace's personal account of sailing on the schooner. Aunt Doris ("Dodie") of St. John's generously gave me access to notes on uncle Bill's diary, the mechanical ships log, and other valuable information. "Dodie" is now a Wilcox, but is the widow of Reg Rowe, my dad's brother and crewman on the *Fronie Myrtle.* Bill Broderick, formerly of St. Brendan's, helped me with a description of a ketch anchor and its historical significance. My brother-in-law, Selwyn Burry, under dad's direction, drew a sketch of the forecastle. I am grateful to the staff of the Newfoundland and Labrador Heritage website for permission to reproduce maps from the Newfoundland Royal Commission 1933 Report (London: His Majesty's Stationary Office, 1934). Their website also provided invaluable information about the Newfoundland Commission of Government. I also wish to acknowledge the valuable content I gleaned from *West Indy Fish – From Fish Out of Water: The Newfoundland Saltfish Trade 1814-1914* by Shannon Ryan published by Breakwater Books in 1986. I must also thank my mom, Dot; my sisters, Nancy, Arlette, Alexia & Monique; and my daughters, Laurieann and Tiffany. Your enthusiasm and boundless interest in my work keeps me writing. To my husband, Terry, I say thank you from my heart for your encouragement, support, and patience during this project. Finally, special thanks to Donna Francis (Editor & Marketing Manager) and the staff of Creative Book Publishing for accepting my book, completing the wonderful design work, and for helping me honour a promise to my dad.

HOME IS THE SAILOR

Home is the sailor, home from the sea:
Her far-borne canvas furled
The ship pours shining on the quay
The plunder of the world.
Home is the hunter from the hill:
Fast in the boundless snare
All flesh lies taken at his will
And every fowl of air.
Tis evening on the moorland free,
The starlit wave is still:
Home is the sailor from the sea,
The hunter from the hill.

A.E. Housman (1859-1936)

"There's a saying
about wooden ships and iron men.
There were a few iron boys around also."
(Max Rowe)

MAXWELL R. ROWE

Maxwell R. Rowe was born on March 16, 1933. In 1953 he married Dorothy Warren from Chapel Arm and together they raised a family of five girls in Chance Cove. Being very close to his father (Will), Max spent his early years as crewman on the schooner *Fronie Myrtle* and later assisted in the family business. Although in later years his work often took him to other parts of the island, Max always looked forward to returning home. He lived life to the fullest and frequently entertained family and friends with his accordion and storytelling. Max passed away on June 3, 2010, but not before he made his unique contribution to *Wooden Ships & Iron Men.*

Suzanne E. Wheeler

Suzanne E. Wheeler was born on April 6, 1954, in Chance Cove, Newfoundland and Labrador. The rocky beach was her favourite playground as a child. She also has fond memories of peering through the openings on her grandfather's wharf and watching the sea life below. *Wooden Ships & Iron Men* was supposed to be her gift to her father, but she would rather say it was his gift to her. Although she will always be a baygirl at heart, she now lives in Grand Falls-Windsor with her husband Terry. They have two daughters, one son in-law, and a very special grandson. Besides writing, Suzanne enjoys church activities, camping, and entertaining.